PostScript printer assembly steps

Step 1   Mount the logic board (chapter 4).

For the LaserJet:
1. Remove LaserJet logic PC board and control panel PCB.
2. Remove excess plastic (screw mounts, cartridge slot edge).
3. Install nylon PC board offsets.
4. Install logic board.

For the NEC and other generic printer engines:
1. Remove excess plastic (screw mounts, cartridge slot edge).
2. Install nylon PC board offsets.
3. Install logic board.

Step 2   Select and build an interface (chapter 4).
- Serial only—baud rate switchable plus interface status LED.
- AppleTalk only—no switch.
- Composite—AppleTalk/Serial switchable with interface LED.

Step 3   Select and add logic board power source. (Applicable to NEC and similar engines only. See chapter 5.)

For the LaserJet:
1. Integral power supply included with machine.

For the NEC and other generic printer engines:
1. Internal power supply from HP or Apple.
2. External supply (+5 volts 3 amps) from Jameco or other source.
3. Construct power supply wiring harness.

Step 4   Install LED displays (chapter 9).
1. On/Ready green.
2. Warmup/Busy yellow.
3. Paper Out/Jam red.

Step 5   Connect and test interface, optional switch, power supply (chapter 10).
1. Check power connections at both source and board connectors.
2. Check Serial I/O interface connections for continuity.
3. Check Video I/O interface connections for continuity.
4. Check computer to printer cabling.

Build Your Own
PostScript®
Laser Printer
and Save a Bundle

Build Your Own
PostScript®
Laser Printer
and Save a Bundle

Horace W. LaBadie, Jr.

Notices

Certain portions of this book appeared in article form in *Computer Shopper* and are reproduced here by permission of the publishers.

Apple®	Apple Computer
Apple IIe®	
Apple IIGS®	
LaserWriter®	
Lisa®	
Mac®	
Macintosh®	
LaserJet®	Hewlett-Packard
PostScript®	Adobe Systems
Commodore 64®	Commodore Business Machines
IBM-PC®	International Business Machines
PC-AT™	
PC/XT™	
PS-2™	

FIRST EDITION
FIRST PRINTING

Library of Congress Cataloging-in-Publication Data

LaBadie, Horace W.
    Build your own PostScript laser printer and save a bundle / by
Horace W. LaBadie, Jr.
        p.   cm.
    Includes bibliographical references and index.
    ISBN 0-8306-4738-4   ISBN 0-8306-3738-9 (pbk.)
    1. Laser printers—Design and construction.   2. PostScript
(Computer program language)   I. Title.
TK7887.7.L33   1991
681'.62—dc20
                                                            91-8706
                                                            CIP

TAB Books offers software for sale. For information and a catalog, please contact TAB Software Department, Blue Ridge Summit, PA 17294-0850.

Acquisitions Editor: Roland S. Phelps
Book Editor: Sandra L. Johnson
Production: Katherine G. Brown
Book Design: Jaclyn J. Boone
Cover Photograph: Brent Blair, Harrisburg, PA.

Contents

Acknowledgments

I wish to thank the editors of *Computer Shopper* for their support, particularly:

Stan Veit, Editor-in-Chief Emeritus
Bob Lindstrom, Editor-in-Chief
Charles Cooper, Senior Editor

Also, I must give credit to Greg Saulsbury of Custom Technology for doing the basic work that led to this project's success.

Thanks also to Susan Moss of Laser Connection.

Introduction

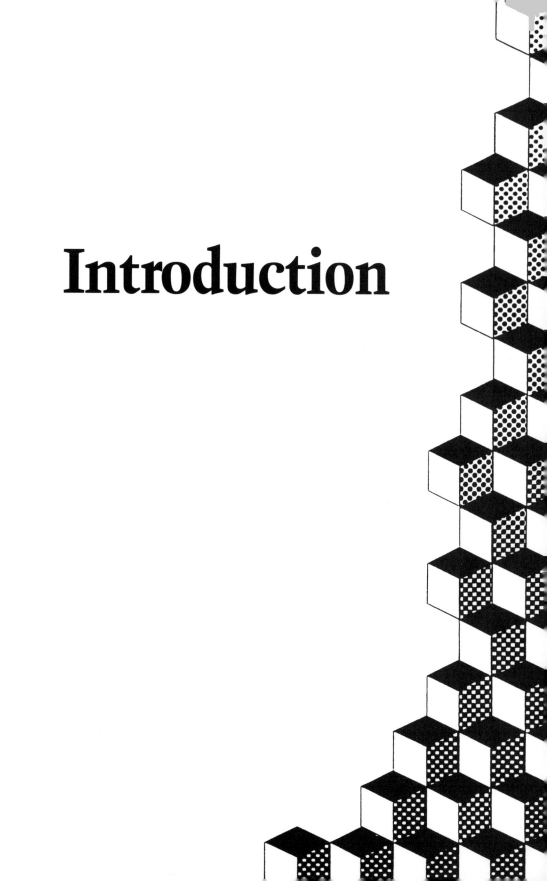

This book explains the process of converting stock Canon CX and SX laser engines to full PostScript printing capability by the use of readily obtainable parts. The project is well within the technical competency of the novice electronics experimenter or builder: No special knowledge of computer architecture is required, and the only aptitude needed is that of wielding a soldering iron in a nonlethal manner. The expenditures of time, effort, and funds are not negligible, but the resultant improvement in the quality of printed output from any computer is so great as to easily justify the respective outlays.

The origin of this book

The origin of the concept of building a low-cost PostScript-capable laser printer is shrouded in the mists of mystery. Like so many legendary ideas, there are many possible candidates for the title of father of the home-brew PostScript printer. Certainly, Don Lancaster, the self-acknowledged PostScript guru, can rightfully claim to be at least foster father of the project, for it was he who first gave the idea currency in his columns for *Computer Shopper* and *Radio Electronics*. However, QMS had already been in the marketplace with their own conversion kits for more than a year when Lancaster announced that it was possible to do-it-oneself without resorting to the QMS products, PS-Jet+ and JetScript.

While Greg Saulsbury of Custom Technology did not invent the idea, he performed the early hard work in exploiting the potential of the notion and was the first to publish coherent plans for the conversion (see the Bibliography for more information). He, in turn, acknowledges the help provided by Chuck Morgan in starting the job. I came into the picture quite late, having purchased Greg Saulsbury's privately printed plans, and I followed the not well-beaten path that they laid. In June 1989, Greg published his revised plans in an article, "Building a Low-Cost PostScript Laser Printer" in *Computer Shopper*. In July 1989, I wrote a brief article, "Boys! Grow Giant LaserWriters in Your Basements!," intended as an addendum to Greg's article in June. I detailed some of the information I had accumulated by experience and filled in some gaps in the plans into which I had fallen during my own execution of the project. The article was eventually published in the January 1990 issue of *Computer Shopper*, and this book is the result of the favorable response which that publication received.

The beginning of personal laser printing

Canon, the Cyclopean Japanese giant, developed the basic mechanism of the laser printer in the 1970s as the foundation of its line of personal copiers. The success of those machines rested largely in the design of the toner cartridge, which contained all of the expendable elements of the copying process and was cleanly and rapidly replaceable by the end user. Of equal importance to the machines' success and to their remarkable low price (a vital factor of that success), but not equally appreciated by the general public, was the design of the laser and its scanning system. It was this design, the very heart of the machine, that made the affordable desktop laser printer an inevitable product. See Appendix A.

The semiconductor laser produces a beam of infrared light, all of one wavelength, in bursts a millionth of a second or less in duration, which can be focused to illuminate a spot as small as 100 microns, or approximately $4/10,000$ of an inch square, giving a theoretical resolution of 2500 dpi. Although the laser is able to reach this fine pitch, a few multiplication operations show that practical printing cannot currently attain this level of resolution due to the limitations imposed by today's micro-hardware. For instance, the ordinary 300 dpi printer gets along quite well with one megabyte of *random access memory* (RAM), representing each dot by one memory *bit* (binary digit). However, the RAM required to address a 2500 dpi bit map on a typical 8×10 inch printed page would be on the order of 780 kilobytes (a *byte* is 8 binary digits or bits; a *kilobyte* is 1024 bytes) per square inch. These requirements make full page images impracticable, even with virtual memory, at current chip densities and processor speeds.

The scanning optics of the engine (Fig. I-1) use low-cost plastic elements.

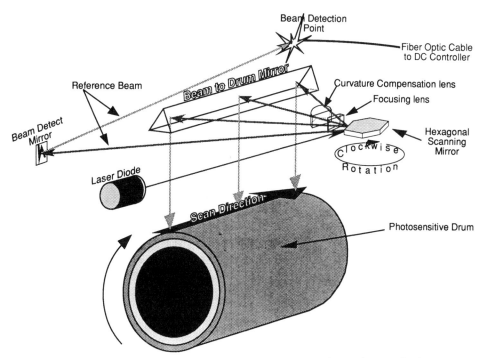

I-1 Diagram of scanning mechanism.

The engine paints the light bursts as pixels across the negatively charged photosensitive drum (Fig. I-2), dispersing the negative charge and attracting the toner particles at the developing station. The aluminum drum is coated with an organic photosensitive material, a characteristic of which is its high conductance (low resistance) when exposed to light, but low conductance (high resistance) in darkness. It is prepared for reception of the image by a rubber wiper blade within the cartridge and by erasure lamps that are embedded in the printer's upper half. These lamps impart a uniform low-resistance state to the drum's surface, allowing any residual charge in the photoconductive layer to be drained. The drum is then given a high voltage negative charge (−600V) over its entire surface. The laser beam serves to dissipate this charge by restoring the low resistance in the areas it strikes. The laser-exposed areas then have a −100V charge, while unexposed areas retain their −600V charge, thus creating the image to which toner is then applied. Toner is attracted to the exposed (lower negatively charged) areas. (See Appendix A for more detail.) The toner particles of a write black engine are a mixture of plastic resin and iron oxide that is projected to the blank page and then bonded to the paper by the heated rollers of the fusion unit, completing the process of printing.

Grouped together in a box, with other more mundane but necessary components, these elements form the basic laser *engine*. All of the laser printers discussed in this book use essentially the same engine. That is the reason that a rather witless printer, such as the HP LaserJet, or even the entirely brainless one, the NEC RPE-4502, can be made into an intelligent PostScript conversant machine.

At this point, it is appropriate to ask, ''Why PostScript?'' Why should you go to the trouble of acquiring PostScript capability?

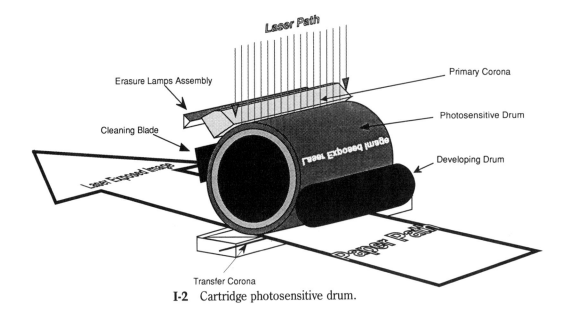

I-2 Cartridge photosensitive drum.

Classes of desktop laser printers

Desktop laser printers with resolutions ranging from 300 to 600 dots per inch belong to that class of imagesetting devices called *page printers*. This category includes machines using laser diode, LED array, and liquid crystal shutter-driven engines (see Appendix A). The class of page printers is represented at the higher resolutions of 1200 and 2400 dots per inch by the print-to-film Linotronic and Compugraphic systems. Page printers primarily differ from the standard computer printers, such as impact and ink jet, in that they compile an in-memory image of an entire page and then transfer that image to paper in one operation, while the pin-headed printers print one line at a time, whether composed of a raster image or alphanumeric characters.

Laser printers are at the current upper limit of personal computer printing. They fall into two basic groups: Those that use or emulate the Hewlett-Packard and those that use or emulate the Adobe PostScript page description language. The Hewlett-Packard based printer is generally cheaper and therefore understandably more numerous than the PostScript-based machine. As you will see, they are virtually identical in all respects except for the language interpreter used in their controllers. Thus, it is possible to pay three or four times more for a true PostScript-speaking printer than for one which emulates the Hewlett-Packard LaserJets. It is possible, but not necessary.

Hewlett-Packard LaserJets

Of the two main camps competing for the laser printer market, that of the Hewlett-Packard (HP) variety is larger. Indeed, from the beginning of personal computer laser printing, the Hewlett-Packard LaserJet series has been the leader in both sales and in the number of imitations spawned. Hewlett-Packard brought the laser printer into the sphere of affordable computer peripheral when it introduced its Series One printer, based upon the Canon LPB-CX model laser engine. The Canon LPB-CX was a smarter variant of Canon's own extremely popular personal copier series. The price was low in comparison to previous laser printers from companies like Xerox, but, at about $2500 from even the discounters, it was still out of the reach of the majority of personal computer users. This prohibitively high price led to the development of the now multitudinous HP compatible copies from the manufacturers of traditional impact printers such as Epson, Panasonic, Okidata, and Alps, and to the collateral development of higher resolution 18, 24, and 27 pin dot matrix ribbon printers, at last bringing high quality printing to the great masses without the high cost.

Quite apart from the price, Hewlett-Packard and its compatibles enjoyed another advantage that led to its domination of the IBM/MS-DOS mainstream: They are in the direct line of descent from the older dot-matrix technology that grew up in an environment saturated by CP/M, the spiritual predecessor of MS-DOS. Because they are largely a superset of an extant technology rather than an altogether different species, the HP and compatibles have a natural adaptive advantage over PostScript printers. Only in their printing method and resolution do the HPs and compatibles differ from their hard copy cousins. At heart, the LaserJet is an upscale dot matrix printer.

At 300 dpi, the LaserJet:

- Offers higher resolution than the most advanced 24 and 27 pin impact printers, which top out typically at 244 dpi.

- Is faster, turning out an average page in about 15 seconds, as opposed to one page every 2 to 5 minutes in highest quality from the impact printers.

- Is quieter, with only its fan and paper feed mechanisms producing any noise at all, compared to the 50 or 60 decibels which emanate from the ordinary pin printer.

Those are its specific virtues. But, like the ubiquitous dot matrix, it creates text by matching the ASCII character codes sent to it with the character sets built into its read-only memory (ROM). As in the lowly dot matrix, those character sets are small in number and are resident only in a few point sizes. The page's text is composed by this translation of individual character codes into predefined bit maps. The text orientation on the page is limited to portrait (vertical) or landscape (horizontal) with a separate bit-mapped character set needed for each of the typefaces and page orientations. Additional typefaces are available by the insertion of font cartridges into a special slot in the logic board, accessed through an aperture in the lid of the printer. HP font cartridges contain generally one type family, but third-party developers have created multi-face cartridges of greater versatility and value. No special effects, such as type rotation, are possible, except as graphic images sent pre-formed from the host device; graphics are essentially raster images, albeit at 300 dpi. Vectored images, such as those used in CAD, are supported, but must be generated by the computer software that sent them to the printer. HP's extensive experience with plotters makes the LaserJet a reasonable choice for such work. Indeed, the latest (mid-year 1990) LaserJet, the Series III, includes plotter functions among its expanded page description language. The Series III also introduces internal outline fonts from Compugraphic, and HP promises more from outside developers in the future.

PostScript is now, and will continue to be, the standard from high end to low end in page description. The Series III is not PostScript compatible, although you can buy an optional 2 megabytes of RAM and PostScript cartridge. HP appears to be moving, like Apple, to avoid the added expense of PostScript licensing while attempting to ape its best features, but it is movement in the wrong direction. Unlike Apple and Microsoft, which are jointly developing a PostScript clone called TrueImage, HP continues to hold out even against PostScript compatibility. Most of the HP compatibles make a virtue of their limitations, boasting high-resolution emulations of the Epson, IBM, and Diablo impact printers, while using the drivers of the impact printers.

PostScript printers

The PostScript laser printer is a very different kettle of fish from the garden pond variety of dot matrix printers. Yes, it is a dot matrix printer in its mechanics, but it is wholly vector based in its page composition, both in text and graphics. (See Appendix A for more about how PostScript works.)

PostScript was specifically designed by John Warnock and others at Adobe to be a computer-based typesetting language. PostScript was not developed out of a previous technology, but was intended to be device independent, rendering any of its commands at the highest resolution offered by the machine in which it resided. Thus, for instance, a file created on a Macintosh and meant to be printed on an Apple LaserWriter, can be transported to any other computer of any type and, when transmitted to a PostScript device, be accepted and successfully rendered, whether the resolution of the destination device be 300 dpi or 2400 dpi.

Because all of PostScript's commands have to do with vectors, any image (text included) that can be mathematically described can be manipulated in a nearly infinite number of ways. Text and graphics can be stretched, rotated, shrunk, twisted, placed in 2- or 3-dimensional perspective, shadowed, or made practically any shade of gray. (See Appendix A.) The only limit to the effects that can be produced in Post-Script is in the user's imagination.

PostScript allows the ultimate freedom with the very minimum of means. If you have the patience and the fortitude, you can, with only the most rudimentary computer and text editor, create any typographic or pictorial effect without actually drawing a single line or dot. Thus a person stranded on a desert isle with only a Commodore 64, a text editor, and a PostScript printer can turn out the same camera-ready artwork as someone drawing at a Sun workstation using the most sophisticated CAD software. Of course, the marooned draftsperson will require magnitudes greater resources of time and brain power to accomplish the same task that could be completed quickly and easily on the minicomputer, but the point is that it can be done.

While actually plotting verbally in PostScript can be woefully inefficient, Post-Script itself is wonderfully efficient. Because a particular text face, for example Times-Roman, exists in PostScript, not as a fixed number of dots or digital bits arranged in a fixed relation one to another, but as a series of mathematical calculations, a text face needs to be described only once for it to be available to the printer at any scale required from 5 to 5000 points. (A *point* is a printer's measure approximately $1/72$ of an inch, which is, not by coincidence, also the screen resolution of the standard Macintosh monitor.)

In PostScript, one description truly does fit all sizes. For example, the characters on the left in Fig. I-3 are bit-mapped Macintosh fonts, the smaller being a 24 point screen font installed in the System and shown dot for dot as it was designed. The larger is the Macintosh QuickDraw rendition of 48 point Times Roman, expanded according to Macintosh ROM algorithms from the 24 point size. The characters on the right in Fig. I-3 are PostScript versions of 24 point and 48 point Times Roman, neither of which is resident in the printer ROM. The type face exists only as a generic set of mathematical descriptions from which any point size can be calculated. If the HP LaserJet uses a type face not in its bit-mapped character set and had to scale its resident bit maps to the requisite size, the results would be similar in aspect to that generated by the Mac's quick-and-dirty ROM, or it would fail to print altogether.

That is the *why* of acquiring PostScript. The rest of this book provides the *how*.

I-3   The difference between bit-mapped (left) and vectored (right) Times Roman.

Chapter 1

The
CX engine

The first eleven chapters of this book focus on the CX engine and how to convert it to a LaserWriter. Chapters 12 and 13 cover the conversion from the SX engine.

A tour of the CX engine printer

The Canon CX laser engine is large. It stands nearly thirteen inches tall, by sixteen inches wide, and eighteen and one-half inches long, weighing in at about 65 – 70 pounds (approximately 30 cm × 41.5 cm × 47.5 cm and 32 kg). Its letter-size paper cassette adds another four inches to the width when inserted. The paper tray into which the printed pages are deposited protrudes a foot from the printer's body. As a desktop peripheral, it is somewhat prepossessing.

Standing in front of the printer shown in Fig. 1-1 with the paper trays in the foreground, the rocker type power switch is located in the left-hand corner, just below the division between the upper and lower halves of the printer. The three conductor power cord plugs into the printer, just around the corner from the switch on the left end. The interface exits about six inches farther back (Fig. 1-2). At the rear corner is a recessed button, with the legend "TEST PRINT" above it. Once the printer has been turned on and has gone through its warm-up cycle, pressing this button forces the processing of a page consisting of a an edge-to-edge grid, useful as verification of the low-level electronic and mechanical integrity of the machine. As a diagnostic, it is used to check scanning and paper alignments. In a pinch, it also makes half of an excellent graph paper.

1-1   The NEC/Canon CX laser engine, front view.

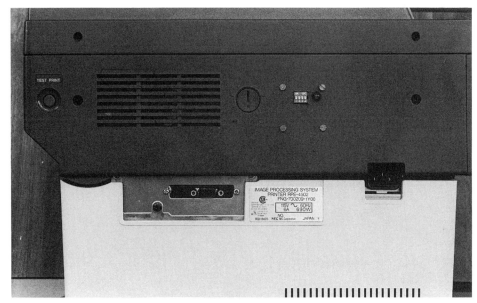

1-2 The CX engine, left end. The power cord in the front corner (right), the interface connector at the rear middle (center), and the TEST PRINT button in the rear corner (left) are standard on all CX engines. The dip switch to the front of the Print Density dial (top center) is user-added and part of project.

1-3 CX laser engine, rear view.

On the back is the manual feed paper slot. On the right end is the cartridge door, in the middle of which is a rectangular window where the cartridge-use gauge is visible when the toner cartridge is in place (Fig. 1-4). At the front right-end corner is a red latch, which operates in an upward motion to unlock the two halves of the printer. The paper cassette from which the blank pages are dispensed fits into a cavity in the bottom front of the printer. The paper exit slot is immediately above. The removable receiving tray is attached by a mortise and tenon pair at either side of the slot. Thus, paper in its trip through the CX engine describes a lazy U pathway. This completes the round-the-printer tour.

1-4 CX laser engine, right end view. Note the latch in the front corner (left), and cartridge usage gauge in small window (top center).

After you lift the red latch, the printer pops open, and the top half swinging upward, clam-shell fashion, exposes the interior of the printer. Immediately in front is a hinged metal plate, covered with a green flocking (Fig. 1-5). The plate can be lifted to reveal the red Teflon-surfaced fusion rollers (Fig. 1-6). These perform the final step in the printing process, bonding the toner to the page with 338°–356° F heat. *Never touch these rollers if the printer has been turned on recently!*

At the right end of the green plate is a flanged aperture, formed by the ends of two metal rails in the bottom of the plate, into which a wand carrying the fusion wiper pad is slipped (Fig. 1-6). The wiper pad is impregnated with a special silicon oil that keeps the rollers clean and lubricated, ensuring that the toner image is bound to the page, rather than offset to the rollers. The wiper pad ought to be changed whenever

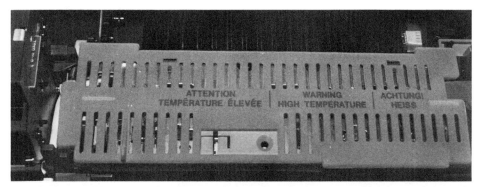

1-5 Inside the CX laser engine. Lid over fusion rollers is shown up, with wiper pad shown in position.

1-6 The cover over the fusion rollers is raised, and the pen points to the cleaning wand.

the toner cartridge is replaced. Behind the fusion assembly is a ridged bed and a thin, nearly invisible wire called the *transfer corona wire*. The purpose of the transfer corona wire is to impart a positive electrostatic charge to the paper before it is drawn into contact with the drum.

To the left, in the front corner, is the printer's main input power supply module. It is protected by a plastic cover, secured on its left side by a single Phillips head screw. Once the screw has been removed, the cover can be pried off to discover the power supply itself. The NEC printer has some unused lugs on the terminal block (just behind the AC power cord's point of entry in Fig. 1-7) that are AC power taps and are controlled by the main switch. It is useful to remember their presence for later reference. To the rear of the power supply is the area occupied by the interface connector(s) as shown in Fig. 1-8. It is also covered by a plastic shield secured by one screw, this one reached from the rear.

1-7 The power supply module shown with cover removed. Note the position of AC taps.

1-8 The interface connector shown with cover removed.

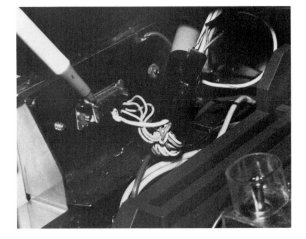

Within the top portion of the printer is where most of the good stuff is to be found. The toner/drum cartridge slides into the top half by way of the swing-down gate at the right. The printer's motor drives a gear train situated in the top, which engages the cartridge mechanism. While not part of the printer itself, the toner cartridge is the heart of the printer and the site of the printing activity. Essentially, the cartridge consists of three parts (Figs. 1-9 and 1-10):

- A tank containing fresh toner.
- The aluminum drum on which the photosensitive coating has been applied.
- A tank for collecting spent or excess toner.

The cartridge is disposable, so Canon does not recommend replenishing toner or replacing worn parts. With the predicted life of a cartridge being between 2500 and

1-9 CX toner/drum cartridge, ready to insert.

1-10 CX toner/drum cartridge, exploded view. Photosensitive drum is in the center, with a fresh toner tank to left and an expended toner tank to right.

3000 pages and the price of a new cartridge being about $80 – $100, the cost per page works out to about 3.2 cents. However, the community of computer users has discovered that, while the toner does become depleted and the spent toner tank does become full, the remainder of the cartridge does not wear out after one use. Methods of refilling the toner reservoir and of emptying the second tank have been developed, and it is not unusual for the useful life of a cartridge to be extended four- or five-fold. Refilling is discussed in Appendix C. Above the cartridge is the lid area, in which the printer's brain is housed.

You have to remove six screws to open the lid. The underside of the lid is the favored mounting site for intelligent controller boards. (For detail, see the HP lid drawing in Fig. 4-4.) When you look down into the lidless printer, you see the DC controller board at the middle front (Fig. 1-11). This is the printer's silicon and fiberglass equivalent of the cerebellum brain, the director of its most basic, autonomic functions, modulating the laser, controlling the scanning of the beam, and determining the vertical and horizontal dots-per-inch density of the printer. As originally shipped, the NEC printer used a 415 dpi controller, while the HP LaserJet and Apple LaserWriter employed a 300 dpi version. The controller boards are easily interchangeable, and some 800 dpi variations have been developed, such as the LaserMAX MX6 controller from LaserMAX Systems (7150 Shady Oak Road, Eden Prairie, MN 55344). The company also markets its own 1000×1000 dpi laser printer with a list price of $7995.

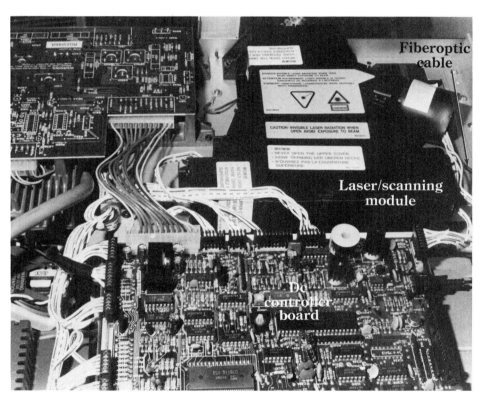

1-11 Under the CX engine's hood. The DC controller is in the lower center. The laser unit is the black box above and toward the center.

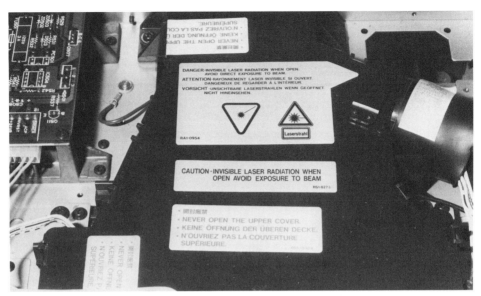

1-12 CX laser unit. DO NOT OPEN!

Toward the rear middle of the printer is a roughly triangular, plastic enclosure (Fig. 1-12). A black plastic cable from the right side of the plastic enclosure extends to a connection on the DC controller board. This enclosure is the *laser scanning assembly*, and the cable is a fiber-optic filament through which the laser transmits a reference beam to the DC controller. The actual laser box should never be opened at any time, but particularly while the printer is in use, due to the danger of eye injuries should the eye be exposed to the beam.

The remainder of the printer's electronics and mechanics need not concern you for the moment.

The convertible derivatives

Certain laser printers offer good platforms for the construction of PostScript printers to cut on cost and labor. The pros and cons of a few printers are discussed here.

Hewlett-Packard LaserJets

The Hewlett-Packard LaserJet One and LaserJet Plus series of printers, being the most frequently encountered versions of the CX engine, form the likeliest platform for the construction of a PostScript printer. Used machines are very often advertised for sale, either in a reconditioned or simply a ''retired'' state, at prices ranging from $500 to $900, depending upon condition. The obvious cautions are attached to buying a used machine that has not been reconditioned: It might have been not only heavily used but actually abused. However, if you get lucky, bargains are available.

Places to look are listed in the Sources section at the end of the book. Shop for the best deal before buying.

Also called the 2686A (a dual cassette version was the 2686D), the HP Laser-Jets, besides their availability, offer other features which make them attractive as the machine with which to start the project. First, because they come complete as printers, the LaserJet controller/interface board has some recoverable value that can help defray the costs of the conversion. Second, and more important to the completion of the project, the printer already contains the auxiliary power supply that is necessary to drive the logic board and its interface, thereby simplifying the conversion process.

Canon LPB-1

The second printer that offers itself for ready conversion is the Canon LPB-1, also called the LPBX or LPB8-1. This is Canon's own early entry into the laser printer market. It went unnoticed in a big way, due to the fact that it was not much more than a very expensive, high-resolution, Epson-compatible printer, and it was quickly overshadowed by HP's much more versatile LaserJet. Stocks of new units were liquidated at $500-$700 each, and some are still showing up occasionally at similar prices. These make excellent vehicles for the PostScript logic board, and, being new, they have their full 100,000 page lives ahead of them. Also, like the HP models, they include the needed power supply. Except for their small numbers, they would be the preferred starting point of the project.

NEC RPE-4502

The last printer to be particularly discussed is the NEC RPE-4502. This printer has a somewhat humble past, and it requires more work to convert it to LaserWriter compatibility than some others. However, it is cheap and comes new out of the box, despite having been manufactured in 1984–85. It was intended to be the hard copy printout portion of a large, complex, and costly facsimile station that consisted of the printer, a 400 dpi flatbed scanner, an 8086 CPU, and modem, all collected in a massive cabinet. The printer itself was configured to print at 415 dpi, about twice the resolution of the normal Group 3 fax machine. This huge assemblage of equipment seems to have amounted to overkill, because it did not leave much room in most offices for a desk, let alone a desktop. The printers and the rest were subsequently sold by liquidators.

Because the NEC printer is the unit most nearly resembling the crude laser engine from which Apple and Hewlett-Packard developed their own printers, anything that can be said of it applies equally to those others. I use it as the basis for the conversion process as discussed in this book. Differences between it and the HP printer as they affect the work are noted where appropriate.

Chapter 2

Apple
LaserWriter
controllers

Price and the logic of its controller board are the two respects in which the LaserWriter differed from the HP printer. The LaserJet listed for about $3000 while the LaserWriter sold for about twice that price. Because the only other appreciable difference between the two machines lay in their controllers, you might wonder how Apple could charge that much and get away with it. That Apple was reportedly paying Adobe a $1000 royalty on each machine shipped had something to do with the price. Apple's fondness for high profit margins and concomitantly high quarterly earnings also played a role in determining the manufacturer's suggested retail price.

LaserWriter One and Plus

But, in fact, the LaserWriter was worth it, or very nearly so. Still, however much it might have been worth the money, it was far beyond the stretch of all but the most plastic of budgets. The LaserJet, with its huge price advantage, soon became the new common standard in high quality personal printing, with the LaserWriter becoming a part of the Macintosh office, a business solution in search of a business problem. Its success came from the high-end users who had smuggled the Mac into the office environment through the postern of the corporate art departments. The upward compatibility of PostScript to the real printshop printers made it possible for all proof work to be done in-house without resorting to costly trips to the Linotronic typesetters. And, much to the surprise of everyone, for a great number of uses, the LaserWriter output could be substituted bodily for the finished copy of those real printers. But that level of use was far removed from the majority of computer owners.

Apple, understandably protective of its intellectual property, keeps the tightest grasp upon its end products of any computer manufacturer. The Apple customer does not so much own an Apple computer as pay for the right to use it. If you need to have equipment repaired, you take it to Apple, or suffer the consequences, suitably dire in nature as befits the offense. Apple uses many proprietary components, and it is loathe, nay, revulsed by the mere suggestion that it ought to supply its end users with the parts which they need to effect their own repairs. The difference between Apple and the Spanish Inquisition regarding deviance from their respective credos would be hard to find.

However, as everyone knows, the only result of Apple bashing is applesauce. Apple Computer goes on in its own way, and it manages very well, thank you.

Built-in fonts

In the half megabyte of ROM of the original LaserWriter are four resident font families, the Adobe Type 1 typefaces Times, Courier, Helvetica, and Symbol (Fig. 2-1), each in standard, bold, italic, and bold-italic faces. Furthermore, each is scalable to any size and infinitely malleable. Type 1 faces are *hinted*, which is to say that they contain algorithms that subtly thicken and alter certain portions of their characters at the ordinary reading point sizes of the 300 dpi printers. In larger sizes, the hints are ignored.

Times is based upon the typeface used by the *Times* of London newspaper. It is a traditional serif face, very readable, and can be used for almost any purpose. Courier is a monospaced face that is based upon the common typewriter character style. It is a serif face, unassuming and unprepossessing. It is used by those who wish to convey the impression that they are excellent typists. Helvetica is an all purpose sans-serif face, deceptively elegant in its simplicity. And Symbol is a catchall typeface, containing all those lovely and exotic squiggles and accents that lend spice to an otherwise dull dissertation. These and other Adobe typefaces gave the computer user a legitimate sense of real typesetting. The difference between the print shop term ''font'' and the Macintosh term ''font'' became blurred, and 12 point Times Roman became endemic.

The LaserWriter Plus could have been dismissed with a nod at Apple's liquidity, except that it was an actual improvement on the LaserWriter. Cosmetically and mechanically identical to the first LaserWriter, the Plus's ROMs swelled to one megabyte, with version 38 of PostScript, correcting some of the more egregious bugs of its antecedent and imposing a new and odious protection upon the Adobe typeface outlines. Also, almost as an afterthought, it added seven new type families to the four originals; three serif faces (Palatino, New Century Schoolbook, and Bookman), two sans-serif (Avant Garde and Helvetica Narrow), and two novelty faces (Zapf Chancery and Zapf Dingbats) filled out the new ROM, and the full eleven-face set became the de facto default series for all PostScript printers thereafter.

In addition to the ROM, the LaserWriter controller boards were populated with $1^1/_2$ megabytes of RAM. This is enough memory to provide space for a receiving buffer, for a downloaded PostScript dictionary comprised of a user-defined shorthand extension of derived functions, a small area reserved for downloaded PostScript fonts, and, by far the largest portion, a 2400×3000 matrix of 7,200,000 individually addressable dots on an 8×10 inch electronic ''page.''

The PostScript commands sent to the printer are captured and interpreted from the ROM. A corresponding bit map is composed in memory, a digital analog of the toner image that will be fixed on the paper page. As is implied here, the interpretation of the commands is made by an onboard processor, an 8 MHz Motorola 68000, the same chip used in the 128K through SE Macintoshes. (The LaserJet controller also uses the 68000 as its CPU, a point that probably has some significance that escapes me.) And there is all the requisite hardware to handle the routine input/output of the data from the host and to the printer's laser. The LaserWriter logic board is nothing less than a single-board computer, called by Apple in 1985, ''the most powerful computer we make.''

2-1 Four Adobe PostScript type families found in LaserWriter I.

AaBbCcDdEeFfGgHhIiJjKkLlMmNnOoPpQqRrSsTtUuVvWwXxYyZz 1234567890-=

!@#$%^&*()_+⁄¤‹›ﬁﬂ‡°·,—± ¡™£¢∞§¶•ªº–≠

ÅåÀˆÀÄâåäãı∫ÇçÎð‰`E^E¨Eéêëè~eÏﬂ©Ó˙È^Ì´Ì¨Íîì ̈~iŸÔ∆ ̇Ò¬ ̄μˆñØø∏πŒœÂ®ÍßÊ†Ë
~U^U`UÜüûù~u◊√„∑Ù≈Á¥Û Ω""''Ú…Æœ ̄≤ ̆≥¿+ This is twelve point Times Roman.

AaBbCcDdEeFfGgHhIiJjKkLlMmNnOoPpQqRrSsTtUuVvWwXxYyZz 1234567890-=

!@#$%^&()_+ ⁄¤‹›ﬁﬂ‡ °·,—± ¡™£¢∞§¶•ªº–≠*

ÅåÀˆÀÄâåäãı∫ÇçÎð‰`E^E¨Eéêëè~eÏﬂ©Ó˙È^Ì´Ì¨Íîì ̈~iŸÔ∆ ̇Ò¬ ̄μˆñØøΠπŒœÂ®ÍßÊ†Ë
~U^U`UÜüûù~u◊√„∑Ù≈Á¥Û Ω" "'Ú…Æœ ̄≤ ̆≥¿+ This is twelve point Times Italic.

AaBbCcDdEeFfGgHhIiJjKkLlMmNnOoPpQqRrSsTtUuVvWwXxYyZz

1234567890-= !@#$%^&*()_+ ⁄¤‹›ﬁﬂ‡°·,—± ¡™£¢∞§¶•ªº–≠

ÅåÀˆAÄâåäãı∫ÇçÎð‰`E^E¨Eéêëè~eÏﬂ©Ó˙È^Ì´Ì¨Íîì ̈~iŸÔ∆ ̇Ò¬ ̄μˆñØø∏π
ŒœÂ®ÍßÊ†Ë~U^U`UÜüûù~u◊√„∑Ù≈Á¥Û Ω""''Ú…Æœ ̄≤ ̆≥¿+ This is
twelve point Times Bold.

AaBbCcDdEeFfGgHhIiJjKkLlMmNnOoPpQqRrSsTtUuVvWwXxYyZz

1234567890-= !@#$%^&*()_+ ⁄¤‹›ﬁﬂ‡°·,—± ¡™£¢∞§¶•ªº–≠

ÅåÀˆAÄâåäãı∫ÇçÎð‰`E^E¨Eéêëè~eÏﬂ©Ó˙È^Ì´Ì¨Íîì ̈~iŸÔ∆ ̇Ò¬ ̄μˆñØø∏πŒœÂ®
ÍßÊ†Ë~U^U`UÜüûù~u◊√„∑Ù≈Á¥Û Ω""'Ú…Æœ ̄≤ ̆≥¿+ This is twelve point
Helvetica.

AaBbCcDdEeFfGgHhIiJjKkLlMmNnOoPpQqRrSsTtUuVvWwXxYyZz

1234567890-= !@#$%^&()_+ ⁄¤‹›ﬁﬂ‡°·,—± ¡™£¢∞§¶•ªº–≠*

ÅåÀˆAÄâåäãı∫ÇçÎð‰`E^E¨Eéêëè~eÏﬂ©Ó˙È^Ì´Ì¨Íîì ̈~iŸÔ∆ ̇Ò¬ ̄μˆñØø∏πŒœÂ®
ÍßÊ†Ë~U^U`UÜüûù~u◊√„∑Ù≈Á¥Û Ω""'Ú…Æœ ̄≤ ̆≥¿+ This is twelve point
Helvetica Oblique.

AaBbCcDdEeFfGgHhIiJjKkLlMmNnOoPpQqRrSsTtUuVvWwXxYyZz

1234567890-= !@#$%^&*()_+ ⁄¤‹›ﬁﬂ‡°·,—± ¡™£¢∞§¶•ªº–≠

ÅåÀˆAÄâåäãı∫ÇçÎð‰`E^E¨Eéêëè~eÏﬂ©Ó˙È^Ì´Ì¨Íîì ̈~iŸÔ∆ ̇Ò¬ ̄μˆñØ

ø∏πŒœÂ®ÍßÊ†Ë~U^U`UÜüûù~u◊√„ΣÙ≈Á¥ÛΩ"""'Ú…Ææ¯≤≥¿+

This is twelve point Helvetica Bold.

```
AaBbCcDdEeFfGgHhIiJjKkLlMmNnOoPpQqRrSsTtUuVvWwXxYyZz
1234567890-= !@#$%^&*()_+ ^A`E^EE~e^I`II~i~U^U`U~u This is
twelve point Courier.
```

```
AaBbCcDdEeFfGgHhIiJjKkLlMmNnOoPpQqRrSsTtUuVvWwXxYyZz
1234567890-= !@#$%^&*()_+ ^AE^EE~e^I`II~i~U^U`U~u This is
twelve point Courier Italic.
```

```
AaBbCcDdEeFfGgHhIiJjKkLlMmNnOoPpQqRrSsTtUuVvWwXxYyZz
1234567890-=  !@#$%^&*()_+  ^A`E^EE~e  ^I`I¨I~i~U^U`U~u
This is twelve point Courier Bold.
```

ΑαΒβΧχΔδΕεΦφΓγΗηΙιϑφΚκΛλΜμΝνΟοΠπΘθΡρΣσΤτΥυςϖΩωΞξΨψΖζ
1234567890-= !≅#∃%⊥&*()_+ ∨⇔⇐⇑⇒⇓◊Υ⟨®∇± ℑ♠≤′%ƒ∞≈…∠↑

ℂ⊥Α   ∫ ≡ ⌊∂™ Ē⊥Ε←Ε   ~ε⌈⊗{♥⌊∥⌈⊥Ι Ī←Ι ~ι∧∣∅🍎⌋〉
ℜ⊨)↓⌟÷≠∈∉Σ♦∣♣⌈⌊~Υ⊥Υ Ȳ   ~υ·℘©•∣⊕∣×⌈∣©®∏™∫⊃→—⌡″⌋≥ℵ√
Τηισ ισ τωελϖε ποιντ Σψμβολ.

ΑαΒβΧχΔδΕεΦφΓγΗηΙιϑφΚκΛλΜμΝνΟοΠπΘθΡρΣσΤτΥυςϖΩωΞξΨψΖζ
1234567890-= !≅#∃%⊥&()_+ ∨⇔⇐⇑⇒⇓◊Υ⟨®∇± ℑ♠≤′%ƒ∞≈…∠↑*

ℂ⊥Α   ∫ ≡ ⌊∂™ Ē⊥Ε←Ε   ~ε⌈⊗{♥⌊∥⌈⊥Ι Ī←Ι ~ι∧∣∅🍎⌋〉
ℜ⊨)↓⌟÷≠∈∉Σ♦∣♣⌈⌊~Υ⊥Υ Ȳ   ~υ·℘©•∣⊕∣×⌈∣©®∏™∫⊃→—⌡″⌋≥ℵ√
Τηισ ισ τωελϖε ποιντ ΣψμβολΙταλιχ.

ΑαΒβΧχΔδΕεΦφΓγΗηΙιϑφΚκΛλΜμΝνΟοΠπΘθΡρΣσΤτΥυςϖΩωΞξΨψΖζ
1234567890-= !≅#∃%⊥&*()_+ ∨⇔⇐⇑⇒⇓◊Υ⟨®∇± ℑ♠≤′%ƒ∞≈…∠↑

ℂ⊥Α   ∫ ≡ ⌊∂™ Ē⊥Ε←Ε   ~ε⌈⊗{♥⌊∥⌈⊥Ι Ī←Ι ~ι∧∣∅🍎⌋〉
ℜ⊨)↓⌟÷≠∈∉Σ♦∣♣⌈⌊~Υ⊥Υ Ȳ   ~υ·℘©•∣⊕∣×⌈∣©®∏™∫⊃→—⌡″⌋≥ℵ√
Τηισ ισ τωελϖε ποιντ Σψμβολ Βολδ.

Chapter 3

Alternatives to Apple

A couple of years after Apple and Adobe created the desktop publishing market ab nihilo (some would say de nihilo), it became apparent that they were on to a good thing. Desktop publishing was hot, and PostScript was as hot as the fusion rollers of the LaserWriters that were translating it into millions of pages of printed copy. Adobe's stock soared in the market, and Apple enjoyed the benefits of the boom, both in respect to its own profits from equipment sales and from the large block of Adobe common stock that it had acquired early in the relationship. The only problem with all this, at least from the viewpoint of the ordinary user, was the prohibitive cost of a LaserWriter. LaserWriter service bureaus offered a partial solution, giving the user access to PostScript on a pay-as-you-print basis, but, at a dollar a page, this was something which could only be used for the final copy, not for experimentation with page layouts and PostScript effects.

Hardware solutions
QMS PS-Jet + and PS-Jet + M

Then QMS came up with the PS-Jet + user-added PostScript interpreters. The PS-Jet + was the first commercially viable means of converting a standard Hewlett-Packard LaserJet into a PostScript machine. It came as a kit, retailing at about $1800. The kit contained an intelligent logic board with 2 megabytes of RAM and the same ROM set as the LaserWriter Plus, mounted in a replacement lid for the printer. Interfacing was accomplished through the LaserJet's standard RS-232 port, and AppleTalk was offered. It was a neurosurgery kit for laser printers, and the result was an Apple-compatible machine that cost, counting the original cost of the Laser-Jet, about $2000 less than a LaserWriter, which Apple was selling for $5999.

This remains the only commercial, user-installable Adobe upgrade for the Canon CX engine. Still, you can accomplish the same ends for less money.

Software emulations

There are always two possible approaches to solving a computer-related problem, either through hardware or through software. The answer can be obtained through either, with tradeoffs or compromises whichever way you choose. The first solution attempted was in hardware, but the cost was the inescapable compromise. So, several companies looked for a software solution.

GoScript

The earliest practical entry was GoScript from LaserGO. GoScript emulated Post-Script without infringing upon Adobe's copyrights. This was not PostScript for the printer, but a PostScript clone for the host. This allowed a relatively inexpensive HP-compatible laser printer to act like a true PostScript device, because the host computer had already digested the PostScript down into a form that it could comprehend.

GoScript and its compeers were handicapped on several levels. First, due to the encryption scheme which Adobe had implemented to make clones impracticable, Adobe Type 1 fonts (and their hints) were not supported. Thus, the standard type faces which were utilized by desktop publishing programs, such as PageMaker from Aldus, were not available to the emulations. Therefore, to make up the difference, so to speak, it was necessary to add third-party typefaces to the package, outline fonts similar in form and function to Adobe's, but unprotected. Of course, this must lead to incompatibilities, due to the inability to use copyrighted font names; and the absence of a replacement font called for by the original PostScript file could result in crashes and unpredictable page composition.

Another handicap lay in the very nature of the solution, that it was based within the host itself and not in the printer. A PostScript interpreter or emulator requires a lot of memory, and consumes even more memory in composing its pages. Therefore, the standard 640K IBM or MS-DOS computer, the target for such an emulator, was an inadequate foundation for the program. Even with extended memory (adding to the cost of the package, by the way), speed was a problem. Software being generically slower than hardware, a software emulation must be slower than its hardware counterpart. And, while the computer was monopolized by the complicated number crunching that such an emulation demands, it was unavailable for other uses. These were the software compromises.

The uncompromising compromise

Eventually, somebody came up with a solution that combined the cost effectiveness of software with the uncompromising speed and hardware independence of a Post-Script-based printer, the LaserWriter transplant.

Thankfully, among the multitudes of microcomputer users are some of the most fervently heretical of all humanity. These do not hate to be told that they cannot do something, they love it. They are certain that there is always something being withheld, some ineffable secret which the cognoscenti might penetrate by dint of inspired hacking. And, more often than not, they are right. Just what makes the LaserWriter special? Well, apart from the controller board, nothing at all. So when, in the course of time and human nature, used LaserWriter boards began to appear on the dark gray market, LaserWriter brain transplants began to occur.

Apple is itself responsible for this state of affairs, for it has adopted the automobile industry's policy of planned obsolescence. No product from Apple is ever sufficient unto tomorrow. The LaserWriter was followed by the LaserWriter Plus, and, as board swaps and ROM upgrades became more frequent, Apple lost control of more and more units, and LaserWriter logic boards began slipping into private hands. The only trouble was, you had to do it yourself with whatever hints or guidance you could track down.

Chapter 4

The
conversion
process

The laserwriter logic board (Fig. 4-1) is large, approximately

18×16 inches. It has three basic sections—memory, logic, and interfaces. Looking at it with the interface connectors to the right, the $1\frac{1}{2}$ megabytes of memory is on the left-hand third of the board, arrayed in banks of 256K dynamic RAM chips. In the center of the board are the ROM chips and the Motorola 68000 CPU with the support chips necessary for data input and output. On the right is the section devoted to the two interfaces, the Video I/O and the Serial I/O, which connect the board to the printing plant and to the host network. With the exception of the ROMs, which are socketed, all chips and other components are soldered to the board.

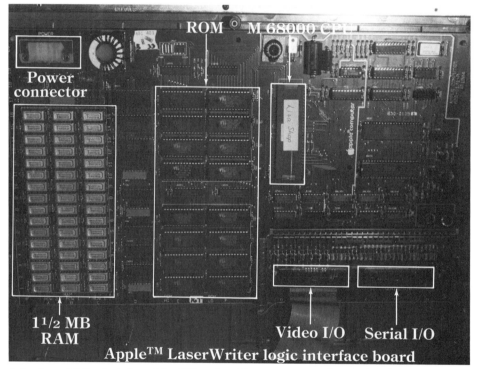

4-1 LaserWriter logic board for CX engine. Power connector is rear left. The left section holds $1\frac{1}{2}$ megabytes of memory. Motorola 68000 CPU and ROM chips are in center. Input/output connectors are on lower right.

The NEC laser engine does not have a native logic/interface board. It was designed simply to capture a raw video raster image generated by the separate Intel 8086 CPU and to print that image, scan line by scan line. It was a slave system. The video signal that it accepted was transmitted to the printer through a port, a large 37-pin D-type connector, found on the left side of the printer. From it, a thick multiconductor video input cable passes around the back of the chassis and up into the top of the printer, where it plugs into the DC controller board by means of a flat IDC (insu-

4-2 The video cable of the NEC engine. The IDC connector need not be disturbed, but the 37-pin D-connector must be removed to make way for the DB-9 of new LaserWriter interface.

lation displacement connector) as shown in Fig. 4-2. This is the simplest form of the Canon CX engine, and therefore the cheapest.

Mounting the controller board

In Fig. 4-3, you can see inside the printer's lid, which is secured by Phillips head screws on either side and at the back. There is clear evidence that the CX engine

4-3 Inside the NEC lid. The plastic screw posts have been removed, as has a portion of the font cartridge slot to make room for the nylon mounting board offsets.

was designed with font cartridge technology in mind, because the knockout along the front is what HP uses for exactly that purpose.

To mount the logic board in the lid, it is necessary to trim some of the plastic that defines the area where the font cartridge was to have been installed. This can be done with an X-acto knife and is probably the only hazardous operation in the conversion. Also, it is necessary to excise the screw mounting posts; the mounting holes of the LaserWriter board do not match the posts' positions, and they raise the board too far from the lid's surface. Once all the superfluous plastic has been cut away, the logic board can be laid inside the inverted lid to obtain a template for locating the board standoffs that will support the logic board in the completed printer. You should mark corresponding positions on the lid with a felt pen for the four holes, one in each corner of the board. Having marked them, remove the board and return it to its protective anti-static bag.

Next, using epoxy glue, the nylon board standoffs should be cemented to the lid in the places marked. Make certain that epoxy is used, because the board is heavy and only epoxy is sufficiently strong to withstand the weight of the board. Once the glue has set, hold the board over the standoffs to check for alignment by sighting through the holes. Small misalignments need not be worrisome, as there is some play in the nylon. Do not install the board at this time, as the glue, though set, might be weakened by movement before it has cured.

The LaserJet lid contains the HP interface board that must be extracted from the printer before the installation of the LaserWriter board can be made (Fig. 4-4). Removal of the lid entails disconnecting the cables that are at connectors J1, J2, and J7 at the back of the board. Next, take out the screws holding both the interface/controller board and the control panel circuit board, and remove the printed circuit boards. The remainder of the mounting procedure is the same as for the NEC engine.

Types of interfaces and their construction

A LaserWriter is useless without some avenue through which data can be acquired for printing. The Apple LaserWriter is provided with two such avenues, the serial and AppleTalk (now LocalTalk) interfaces. The interface is selected and the communications protocol is set by a rotary switch. Apple has established 1200 baud, 9600 baud, and AppleTalk's 230,400 bits per second (230.4 kilobaud) as the ordained rates of data transfer.

In the beginning, Apple attempted to lead everyone to believe that the only proper device to be connected to a LaserWriter was a Macintosh or Lisa/Mac XL operating on an Apple-cabled AppleTalk network. This was patently nonsense on the face of it, because the serial interface was there to be used. Apple also discouraged the public from the idea that other rates of speed could be selected than those which were selected by the switch. The public has since been disabused of both notions, largely through the pertinacity of Don Lancaster, who has demonstrated that any computer can be connected to a LaserWriter at either port, and that the serial baud rate of the 9600 baud setting is software controlled and controllable. He has attained 57,600 baud from the game port of an Apple IIGS, and he avers that even higher speeds are not impossible. (See his article ''Ask the Guru'' in the April 1989 *Computer Shopper*, pp. 412-414.)

The point of this discussion is that this project requires that you as the builder must construct the interface of your choice, either serial or AppleTalk, but that the AppleTalk version is the easier to make and the more useful choice. It might come as a surprise to those who are converting the HP printer that, when the LaserJet logic board is removed, the interfaces go with it, but that is the case. The NEC printer has only the straight through video interface that must be replaced. The requisite interfacing options for the LaserWriter board are described hereinafter.

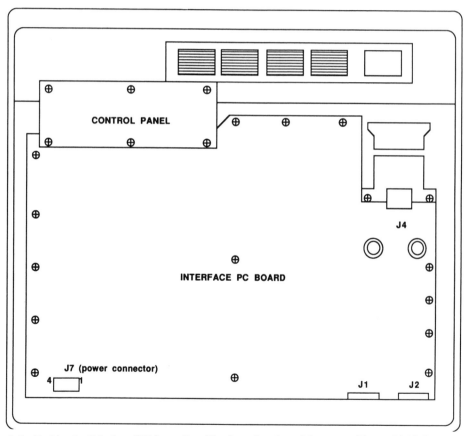

4-4   Inside the lid of an HP LaserJet. The interface board is covered by a shield that must first be removed.

Serial

The wiring of a serial-only port requires that a number of lines be used that are not required for the simpler AppleTalk interface. It is conventional to build this interface if the printer is to be used by a computer other than a Macintosh, Lisa, or Apple IIGS, although any of those machines can use a LaserWriter as an unadorned serial peripheral at 1200 or 9600 baud. In general, however, serial connection to a Mac is not efficient; the AppleTalk mode is both transparent and fast and is to be preferred. For everybody else, however, serial is the only way to go, barring the installation of an AppleTalk network interface card into an IBM PC or PC clone.

Externally, the serial interface is terminated by a DB-25 or DB-9 connector (Figs. 4-5 and 4-6). This is where the cable from the host computer plugs into the printer. (Those cables are described in a subsequent section.) The other end of the serial interface is formed by a 34-pin female IDC (shown in Fig. 4-9 later) which plugs into the LaserWriter logic board itself, using the flat, male connector marked Serial I/O and found at the front, far right portion of the board. The IDC is keyed to fit the Serial I/O to prevent misorientation: there is a raised ''key'' on the IDC which acts as a guide, and a similarly placed receiving slot will be noted in the top of the Serial I/O connector; matching them ensures the correct alignment. Plugging the interface cable in upside down will not damage the board, but it will prevent the board from executing its internal self-test on start-up.

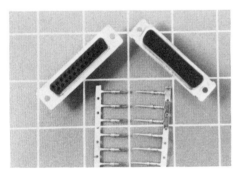 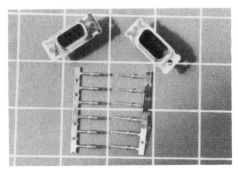

4-5 Common RS-232C DB-25 connectors, male (left) and female (right). The female is used most often as the printer connector. Newer PS/2 and EISA computers have substituted the DB-9. Adapters are available, or a printer cable can be wired accordingly, replacing the DB-25 with the DB-9. See the following section on computer cabling.

4-6 Common DB-9 connectors.

The mode switch of the LaserWriter performs very simply. The communication protocol of the ports, whether AppleTalk or serial, is determined by the state of two lines, 13 and 15, of the Serial I/O during power up. The switch serves to engage those lines to ground or to leave them open, with the communications mode set by comparison to a ROM table that translates as shown in Table 4-1.

Table 4-1. Communications modes.

Line 13	Line 15	Mode
open	open	AppleTalk
open	grounded	Diablo 630
grounded	open	9600 baud
grounded	grounded	1200 baud

The mode to be used by the LaserWriter is determined by comparing the conditions of Lines 13 and 15 to Table 4-1. For the wiring of the switch shown in Fig. 4-7, see the section for the multi-purpose interface.

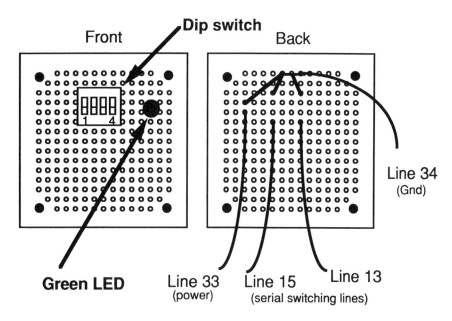

**Mode Switch and Diagnostic LED
mounted on perfboard**

4-7 A diagram for the mode switch and indicator LED.

Table 4-2. Wiring table for RS-232C-only interface.

DB-25	pin 1/SW	SW	SW	pin 2	pin 3	pin 4	pin 5	pin 6	pin 20
IDC 34	pin 34	pin 13	pin 15	pin 17	pin 19	pin 21	pin 23	pin 25	pin 27

From Table 4-1, it is apparent that the default setting for interfacing is Apple-Talk. That is, if no switch were provided, the printer would automatically boot up in the AppleTalk mode every time power was applied. This is indicative of Apple's corporate prejudice, which is both uncomplicated and obvious. However, if one possesses more tolerant views of computers from other folds, then it is compulsory to make provision for their connection by adding a switch. That anything other than AppleTalk is possible must be applauded as a magnanimous concession by Apple.

Besides lines 13 and 15 of the Serial I/O, a serial-only interface uses lines 17, 19, 21, 23, 25, 27, and 34. Line 34 is to ground and can be used to switch lines 13 and 15 between the open and low states. The relation of the 34-pin IDC to the DB-25 of the interface is shown in Table 4-2.

With a four-position (four-switch) DIP switch and Table 4-2, a suitable interface can be constructed without much trouble, as is shown in Fig. 4-7. As a bonus, you can incorporate a green LED into the interface to serve as a reassuring start-up index—on powering up the printer, the LED will light up for a couple of seconds and then will shut off, showing that the logic board is functional. If it remains on, then you have a malfunction, possibly relating to a low voltage condition for the board. A suggested position for mounting the switch is shown in the photographs in Fig. 4-2 and in Fig. 4-16.

AppleTalk

An AppleTalk-only interface is simplicity itself. It engages all of four lines and a ground. As discussed in the previous section, it requires no switch whatsoever. The printer is as happy as the clam that it looks like when opened to run always as an AppleTalk device. The pin assignments are as found in Table 4-3.

Table 4-3. AppleTalk (LocalTalk)-only interface wiring.

DB-9	pin 4	pin 5	pin 8	pin 9	pin 1	ground
IDC 34	pin 7	pin 9	pin 6	pin 8	pin 34	ground

The maximum economy of this interface is appealing. It presents no mysteries and no problems. It has everything except its parochialism to recommend it. If every conceivable computer were an AppleTalk device, then it would be the perfect interface. Of course, not even every Apple Computer computer is an AppleTalk device, so that notion is empty.

Multi-purpose

The fact is, that even Apple Computer lives in the real world, however much some of its policies might seem to affirm the contrary, and the LaserWriter must accommodate machines other than those manufactured by Apple. This makes good business sense, considering that the great majority of personal computers do not bear the Apple logo. And it makes good sense that the interface that is most useful should be the one which is most elegant as well. In principle, one port is all that is needed, the DB-9 connector designated for AppleTalk by Apple. When the printer's mode switch is set to any of the non-AppleTalk baud rates, the AppleTalk port assumes the character of a simple serial port. In the genuine LaserWriter, the two ports can serve as dual serial interfaces, with each being polled by the printer for incoming data, and priority being assigned to the first active port, while the second port is sent the "printer busy" message until the first job is completed. To choose to build either one or the other exclusive interface is, therefore, foolish. Why have just one when, for the same effort, it is possible to have both in the same port?

A composite AppleTalk/serial interface is nothing more than an elaboration of the standard four-line AppleTalk-only port. All that is added is the switch that was constructed in the section dealing with the serial-only interface. By importing that switch to the AppleTalk port, you obtain complete flexibility in interfacing. Any computer with a serial port or any AppleTalk-equipped computer can become the host for the same printer. You run the minimum number of lines and, therefore, the minimum risk of failure, for the fewer the points of connection, the fewer are the sources of potential problems. Pinouts for the interface are in Table 4-4.

Table 4-4. Composite AppleTalk/RS-232 interface wiring.

DB-9	pin 4	pin 5	pin 8	pin 9	SW	SW	pin 1
IDC 34	pin 7	pin 9	pin 6	pin 8	pin 13	pin 15	pin 34

Fabricating the interface cables

The fabrication of the actual interface cable proceeds as follows. Working with the NEC engine, remove the back and left end case panels from the top half of the printer. The screw positions are shown in the earlier photographs. The lid should already have been removed for fitting of the logic board; consult the previous section if this has not been done. Open the printer, and remove the toner cartridge. In lower half of the printer, on the right side behind the power supply module, locate the plastic cover that protects the interface connector. You should see a single screw to remove. After taking off the cover, the interface connector can be unfastened by loosening the screws at either side. The screw attached to the chassis ground wire must also be removed. When the connector is free of the case, thread it out the rear of the printer and up through the top. The other end of the cable is plugged into the DC controller board at the front right hand corner of the printer's top. Unplug the cable.

Remove the DB-37 connector from the one end. The wire clamp can be pried off, as can the plastic cap, allowing the cable to be separated from the connector shell. Note that the wires are in colored pairs. The two gray wires that had been grounded on the frame are lines 33 and 34. Cut off the crimp-on ring lug and then begin counting lines. Having identified the lines to be used from the tables in this chapter, separate them by slicing through the flat sheathing and strip off about 1/4 inch of the insulation from each. Twist the strands and then tin each wire. Crimp on the pins for the DB-9 female connector to the tinned wire ends, making certain of a good mechanical connection, and heat the pins with the soldering iron until the solder of the tinned wires melts. When cool, insert them into the numbered holes of the crimp shell of the connector.

Next, splice and solder 15-inch extension wires on to lines 13, 15, 33 and 34, adding heat shrink insulation. (Heat shrink tubing contracts when subjected to a flame or other high heat source.) Run these wires to the board on which the switch and LED have been assembled, and solder them in place where shown on the rear of the board. Line 33 provides power to the LED when the cable is finally plugged into the Serial I/O. The longer of the LED's "legs" or leads is the *anode*, to which the positive voltage of line 33 is wired (Fig. 4-8). Except for mounting the connector and switch on the end of the printer's case, the interface work is completed.

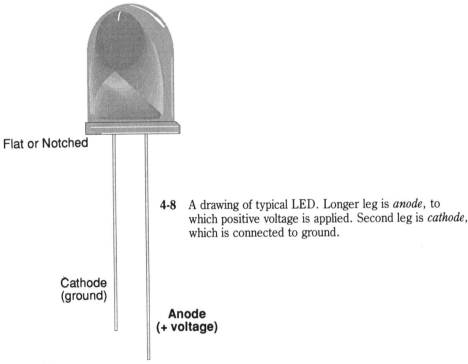

Flat or Notched

4-8 A drawing of typical LED. Longer leg is *anode*, to which positive voltage is applied. Second leg is *cathode*, which is connected to ground.

Cathode
(ground)

**Anode
(+ voltage)**

Lastly, it is necessary to replace the cannibalized video cable. This is done quickly and easily by making a new cable from ordinary 36 conductor ribbon cable (34 conductor cable is available by mail order—see Sources) and two 34 position IDCs, leaving unconnected, or removing entirely, the two unused lines of the cable. Be careful not to expose the adjoining wires of the cable when separating the two excess lines from the others. (See Table 4-5 for video signals/pins.)

Table 4-5. J-202 connector pin assignments.

Pin	Signal	Signal	Pin
1	Reserved	Reserved	2
3	Beam detect ($-$)	Beam detect ($+$)	4
5	Printer power ready	Printer power ready return	6
7	Ready	Ready return	8
9	Vertical sync required	VSREQ return ($-$).	10
11	Status busy	Status busy return	12
13	Status command	Status command return	14
15	System clock	System clock return	16
17	Command busy	Command busy return	18
19	Print	Print return	20
21	Vertical sync power	Vertical sync return	22
23	Controller power ready	C P ready return	24
25	Video signal ($-$)	Video signal ($+$)	26
27	Reserved	Reserved	28
29	Not connected	Not connected	30
31	NC	NC	32
33	Signal ground	Signal ground	34

Ribbon cable is usually gray or blue, solid colored on the bottom, striped on the top. The three parts of an IDC are the header, the ribbon retainer, and the strain relief that snaps over the retainer (Fig. 4-9). On one side of the IDC is a triangle that marks the location of pin 1 (Fig. 4-10). All of the odd-numbered pins are on that side of the connector; if the saw-like teeth on the top are examined, you will see that they are in pairs and that the pairs are in two staggered rows. When the ribbon cable is placed on top of the connector, the teeth penetrate or displace the plastic insulation around the separate lines of the cable and establish contact between the pins and the wires. Because the rows are staggered, adjacent lines are not numerically in sequence and are fully isolated from their neighbors.

To make the connection, special crimping pliers are available, as well as crimping vises, which accept dies for variously numbered pin headers. However, all that is really necessary is a small, flat-bladed screwdriver. Lay the cable (stripes up) over the connector's teeth, with about $1/8$ to $1/4$ of an inch of cable extending beyond the edge of the IDC. It should be possible to begin the puncturing of the insulation by merely pressing down on the cable with your fingertips and then snapping the retaining cap over it, but a finished cable cannot be made so simply.

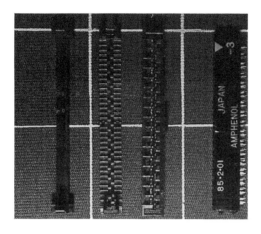

4-9 Typical 34-pin IDC cable connectors. From right side, the three parts are the strain relief, the cable cap, and the connector itself, shown head-on and in profile.

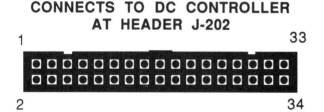

**CONNECTS TO DC CONTROLLER
AT HEADER J-202**

1

33

2

34

4-10 IDC pin placement for video cable. Top has serrated teeth in staggered rows to pierce cable.

It is absolutely necessary that all of the teeth entirely penetrate the cable and protrude from the top. With the retaining cap off, press the screwdriver tip down on the cable lengthwise between the two rows of teeth, making certain that no teeth are bent or broken. (See Fig. 4-11 through Fig. 4-14.) If any teeth are damaged, discard the connector and start again with a new one. Having compressed the cable between the rows, move to the side from which the cable exits along its greater length. Placing the tip of the screwdriver against the outside of the pins, as defined by the cable wrapping over them, apply pressure to the cable with the flat of the screwdriver, driving the cable down against the top of the connector, moving from end to end of the connector until all of the teeth on that side show through the top of the insulation. Do the same on the opposite side, where the cable end overhangs the edge of the IDC. If the procedure has been satisfactorily completed, then each of the teeth of the connector should be clearly visible, and each of the lines of the cable should form a firm electrical connection with its respective pin. Clamp the retainer over the cable until it locks flush with the bottom of the connector. Next, move to the other end of the cable, making certain that it is not twisted and that the stripes are still up.

Repeat the assembly of the other IDC to the cable, preserving the line relationships end to end; that is, make certain that line 1 on the right hand connector is connected to line 1 of the left hand connector. Lines 35 and 36 should be vacant or missing.

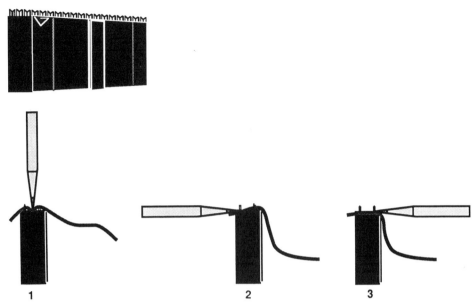

4-11 After manually pressing cable down on connector teeth to pierce cable, (1) use the tip of a small flatblade screwdriver to compress center area between rows, (2) then move to outside edge, working with the flat of blade. (3) Finish by repeating actions of step 2 on the inner edge.

4-12 Attaching ribbon cable to IDC using a flatbladed screwdriver. Start in middle...

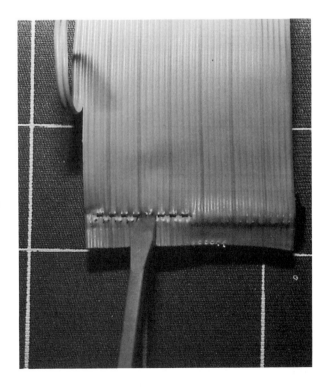

4-13   ...move to outside edge...

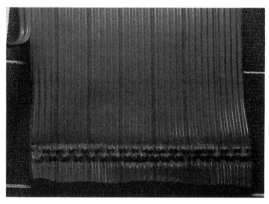

4-14   ...and finish on inside edge.

The last step is to apply the strain relief to each connector by looping the cable back over the connector and snapping the plastic cap down across it until it clicks into place on the connector's ends (Fig. 4-15). This prevents the cable from being pulled loose from the connector. The completed cable then can be plugged into the Video I/O of the logic board and the 34-pin header J-202 on the DC controller board. The keying of the connectors should match that of the headers.

LaserJet differences

On the LaserJet, the cable (HP part number SG4-6108-000CN) that is plugged into the DC controller board at header J-202 can be used without any modification, except for the end that plugs into the LaserWriter logic board at the Video I/O connector. The end that plugs into the LaserWriter logic board must be reversed, with

4-15   Finished cable with connector cap in place.

the IDC rotated 180° (and the raised key facing down instead of up) before being placed into the Video I/O slot (Fig. 4-16). The correct alternative is to remove the IDC and reattach it with the opposite orientation, but the IDC can be forced if laziness, impatience, or indifference preclude that action.

If the LaserJet that is being converted had been furnished with the standard serial interface, the cable that was used by the now-removed board can be adapted to serve as the LaserWriter interface cable. It is necessary to remove, at the least, the connector from the inner end of the cable and to wire a new connector according the scheme given here. This suffices only for the RS-232 interfacing, but an AppleTalk-only or a combination interface needs new connectors at both ends, as described in the applicable paragraphs.

Fitting out of the Video I/O and Serial I/O interface cables is the core activity of the conversion. Some important ancillary threads need to be tied off, however, before the printer can be put into service.

The interface cable should be fed out the rear of the printer and routed to the left end of the printer; do this by reversing the order of its removal. Reposition it through the path from which the old connector was taken. Depending upon the printer and the connector in use, it might be necessary to fashion a filler plate to fit the new connector to the opening. This can be made from a piece of scrap plastic, using the connector shell as a template for the holes. The filler plate should be fastened to the case, and the connector then bolted to the filler.

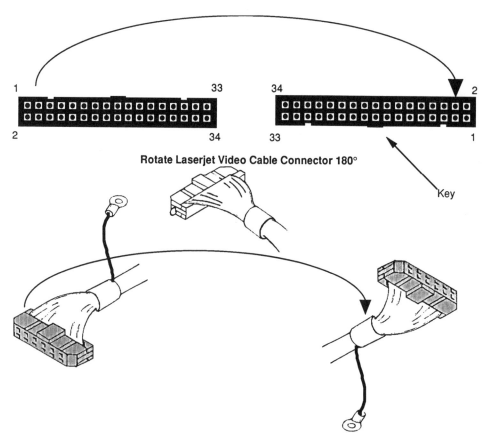

4-16 Correct orientation of LaserJet cable to LaserWriter logic board connector is obtained by flipping the cable over to place key on bottom.

The switch, if present, should be mounted at this time. The left end panel is the most convenient spot, with the switch's PC board and wires are threaded out through the chassis and attached to the panel with self-tapping screws. You need to cut a rectangular opening for the switch and to drill a $1/4$ inch hole for the LED, as well as pilot holes for the screws (Fig. 4-17). An X-acto knife is the best tool for the cutting, and an electric drill with a $1/4$ inch speed bit serves for the drilling. The LED aperture and a $1/16$ inch bit should be used for the pilot holes. The second half of the dual PC board makes the best template for marking the various incisions and drilling points. Install the LED mount into the $1/4$ inch hole and then carefully snap the PC board into place, making certain not to break the leads of the LED. The screws will draw the board tight against the panel. The panel can then be reattached to the printer body. Lastly, the cover for the interface connector can be returned to its place, although it might be more convenient to leave it out temporarily in the event of problems.

4-17 Close-up of mounting position of mode switch.

Next is the question of a power supply. The power connector of the LaserWriter board is in the rear left corner of the board. It accepts the LaserJet power supply cable (two brown and two blue wires ending in a four-pin Molex shell) without modification, but you must add an auxiliary power supply and fashion a wiring harness to serve the logic board if it has been installed in the NEC printer.

Chapter 5

Power supplies

The laser engine, as it was shipped from Canon to the original equipment manufacturers such as Apple and Hewlett-Packard, contained a 690 watt switching power supply rated at 6 amps. (The Hewlett-Packard LaserJet 2686A uses an 850 watt, 6.6 amp main supply, while the 2686D uses a 6.8 amp supply.)

Power requirements

A 690 watt power supply is a relatively robust power source for any computer peripheral, the average personal computer getting by on less than 200 watts. For the laser printer, it is inadequate beyond the draw of the engine itself. This means that, after the Canon supply serves the laser, the paper feed mechanism's motor, the fan, the fusion heating assembly, and the electronics that modulate the laser and produce the image on the drum, nothing remains to power an added interface board. The Apple LaserWriter logic board alone, for instance, is rated as requiring + 5 volts at 3 amps, compelling Apple to provide a supplemental power source for their board. Hewlett-Packard has done the same for its printers. In converting a printer to PostScript, it is helpful, therefore, if this secondary power supply is already part of the printer, but you have other options if one is not present.

Integral

The HP LaserJet contains the needed secondary power supply for the logic board (Fig. 5-1). Depending upon how you have mounted the logic board, the cable might or might not reach the Molex connector of the board. If it does not, then the wires can be extended by cutting the four leads of the power cable and splicing in wires of the same gauge, using wire nuts or solder joints with heat shrink insulation to make the splices (Fig. 5-2).

User added

The NEC engine requires the addition of a logic board power supply. This can be done either externally or internally, depending upon the power supply selected (Fig. 5-3). It is not important which method of mounting is chosen, although the internal mounting is the more esthetically pleasing of the two.

Internally, you have two options. One option is the LaserJet 2686A interface power supply, obtainable from Hewlett-Packard as three discrete units. These units are the interface power supply printed circuit board, part number RH3-2004-000CN; the interface power supply transformer, part number RH3-0014-000CN; and the line filter, part number RF1-0190-000CN, or the LaserWriter power supply, available from Pre-Owned Electronics or another Apple parts dealer for about $199. Figure 5-1 shows the space into which the various assemblies fit in the printer's pedestal and the connections between the terminal block and the line filter, the filter and the transformer, and the transformer and the PC board. The final connection is achieved by running wires from the two +5 volt outputs and from the two grounds to the logic board.

Externally, you have numerous possibilities. In theory, any power supply with a rated capacity of +5 volts at 3 amps should work. This is not always the case in practice, however, because ratings are, in generous terminology, nominal. Three amps might mean 3 amps with no load, but it can also mean 2 amps under load. The same can be said of the voltage under load. Five volts does not always mean 5.0 volts: it can mean 4.9 volts, or 4.75 volts, or even 4.5 volts. Luckily, most electronic devices are very forgiving when it comes to voltages and current. Most electronic devices generally tolerate a variance from the norm, even to the extent of 5%, but the LaserWriter board is something of a strict constructionist. It demands the full 5 volts at 3 amps. Like the Chief who dined with the President, it believes that a "little too

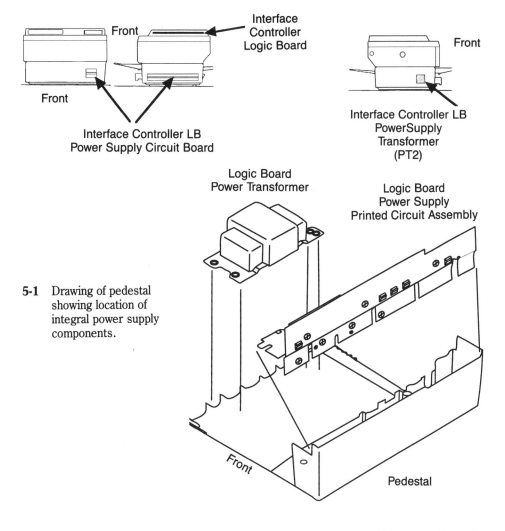

5-1 Drawing of pedestal showing location of integral power supply components.

5-2 LaserWriter logic board power connector with pin locations.

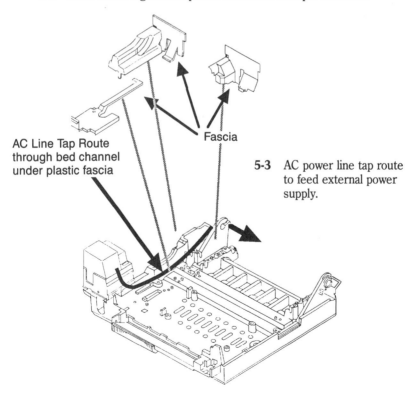

AC Line Tap Route through bed channel under plastic fascia

Fascia

5-3 AC power line tap route to feed external power supply.

much is just enough for me.'' Therefore, you would be prudent to have some margin for manufacturer's exaggeration built into your calculations as power supplies are being evaluated for their suitability to the purpose. A 5 amp supply would probably be the safest choice, because it is large enough to handle the draw of the board without falling below the threshold of 3 amps, yet it is not large enough to represent a mortal hazard to the board's circuitry in the event of an accidental short or power surge. Some switching supplies are of a type that do not function unless they have a drain upon their output terminals. A dummy load must, therefore, be applied across the vacant outputs to ground in order to obtain a steady output from the terminals to be used for the board. Some wire wrapped resistors can be used for this purpose. Either a linear or switching supply will suffice, although the switching supplies are generally smaller and lighter. Although a supply that utilizes large capacitors serves well insofar as it provides some stabilization for the current flowing to the board, those same capacitors take longer to discharge when power is shut off than do the smaller types, and this can prove dangerous, both to you and to the printer. In such a situation, a short can occur even after the power has been turned off. Some capacitors can take up to 30 seconds to fully discharge their load after power to them has been withdrawn. (See the following section on Overpowering.)

One supply that appears to meet the specifications is the Jameco 4 channel switching power supply, part number FCS604A, priced at $44.95 in the Jameco 1990 catalog (Fig. 5-4). The spec sheet for this supply shows that the +5 volt output is adjustable between 4.5 and 5.5 volts with a current range from 1 to 5 amps, with a momentary capacity of 7 amps. Ripple (*ripple* is the wave distortion that occurs during AC cycling) is stated not to exceed 30 microvolts peak to peak, and maximum power is 55 watts. The ability to vary the voltage is important, due to the demands of the board for a full 5 volts, and the 5 amp current is outside the nominal draw of the LaserWriter board.

This supply has been used successfully by Greg Saulsbury in his projects. My experience with it, however, has been disappointing. The first sample that I purchased was of poor workmanship: Its circuit board had been clumsily hand soldered, as if to repair some broken traces, and the potentiometer that adjusted the voltage had a defective wiper and one lead cracked. The cumulative effect of these defects was a ripple measured at more than 300 microvolts and a totally baffling unresponsiveness from the printer. The power supply was replaced by Jameco, but the results were not much more promising. The printer worked, but sporadically, with not much pattern to its performance. Noise was obvious. A third supply of different manufacture was substituted and finally brought the printer reliably on line.

Noise

Some power supplies, then, while perfectly adequate in terms of amperes and voltage, might be unusable for other, more arcane reasons. For instance, if the power

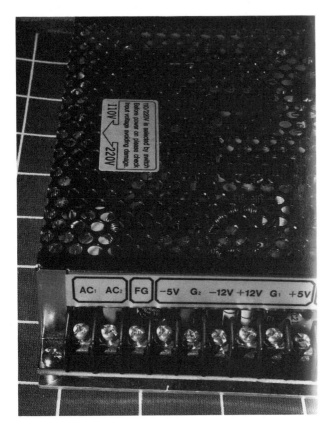

5-4 Jameco four-way
switching power supply.

supply generates an excessive amount of ripple, this can lead to the propagation of interference or noise within the electronic components of the printer. The noise is not audible noise, but spurious digital signals that can confuse and even disable the printer's logic. In practice, the noise is likely to manifest itself as garbling of the data transferred between the host and the printer over the serial interface. The symptoms are easy to recognize: The printer needs longer to receive a file, and it echoes back garbage to the host computer's monitor. Sometimes, after a file has been sent, the printer looks as though it were processing the data, but, actually, it is making mental paper dolls out of the file before drifting off to cloud Cuckoo-Land. If such a pattern of behavior appears, the first place to look is at the power supply serving the board. Replacing it with a clean supply almost always removes the interference. Some ripple is unavoidable and can be tolerated by the system. However, the noisier the power supply is, the more degraded the printer's performance at the higher data transfer rates will be. Sadly, not even a perusal of the specifications can guarantee that the noise level will be within tolerance. Only actual use shows the problem, unless you first attach a prospective supply to an oscilloscope and look for extraneous peaks in the waveforms that can be isolated as high-frequency noise.

Overpowering

Overpowering is the result of putting too much current into a circuit. The board with which I began the project had a hidden defect: Some of the resistors in the resistor packs, the clusters that sit across the Serial and Video input/output lines, had been subjected to a line surge or short and had been badly carbonized or burnt at some point in the board's history.

Carbonization produces increased resistance, and increased resistance requires increased current to overcome it. I found that a 3 amp supply would get no response whatsoever from the board, and a 5 amp supply would provide only the false encouragement of a test page. When the current was increased to 7 amps, the printer worked without any noticeable hesitation. To all appearances, the board was simply outside the normal Apple specifications, which would account for its presence in the used parts market. The way that I discovered the hidden defect is one of those stories that is painful to recall.

The power supply I was using contained a massive capacitor as one of its principal components, and the supply's output was as smooth and regular as I could wish. It flattened out line fluctuations and delivered clean, unvarying power. All would have been well had I not decided, as people do, to make some refinements to the arrangement. These refinements involved disconnecting the power supply from the logic board. I turned off the printer, waited about ten seconds to allow the supply to discharge, and then set about removing the wiring harness. In so doing, I accidentally shorted one of the lines against the power supply case. Two things happened instantaneously and simultaneously, at least in relativistic terms: One, the short sent a surge through the logic board and out its interface, through the serial cable to the computer and into the computer's RS-232C port, zapping both the LaserWriter's and the computer's interfaces indiscriminately; and two, a queasy blow hit me in the abdomen as I heard the sizzle and crack of the shock, and I realized what had probably occurred.

The damage was confined to the interfaces, but it was expensive. It was during the repair that I found out that the filters (resistor packs) had been damaged previously. The service technician could not bring the board up to print a test page, although I had been able to coax one from it, despite that the interface was dead. Then I mentioned that the board had never worked at the specified 3 amps, but had always needed at least 5 amps even to agree to print a test page. This led to the replacement of the filters, which immediately brought the board within the normal power draw of the specifications. Obviously, at some time, the resistor packs had been subjected to a sizable jolt and had been burned without being destroyed. With the hindsight of an eagle, it then became obvious that the short would not have happened had the damaged resistors been replaced following that first incident, because it would not have been necessary to use an overpowered supply to overcome the added resistance.

You can extrapolate several lessons from this sorry episode. One, have the LaserWriter board tested at the time of purchase by a competent technician in order to be certain that it is functioning within its specifications. Do not accept the statement, "It prints a test page," as proof that the board is in good order and is working. Printing a test page proves only that the board is capable of sensing the condition of lines 13 and 15 and of printing a test page. Printing a test page does not ensure that it is capable of doing anything useful, such as printing your own files, for instance. Have sample files downloaded and printed in both the serial and AppleTalk modes—that is the only sure test of the board.

Two, never overpower the board. The consequences of disregarding this lesson can be disastrous (and dear, needless to say). If the board does not work at 5 or less amps, then it is seriously sick and needs to be sent to a service shop. It will cost to have it fixed, but it will cost more to have it and your computer both repaired later.

Three, if at all possible, use AppleTalk cabling, unless you are very, very strong-stomached and fat-walleted. Each AppleTalk connector contains a small inductor coil that serves to dampen any line surges and spikes that might be transmitted along the network. If the network is not so protected, then there is every likelihood that an accident will wipe out every node on the network.

Whichever power supply is used, the wiring scheme is the same. The LaserWriter logic board has a four-pin Molex style connector at the left rear corner, when viewed from above with the interface connectors to the right. A toroidal inductor coil is to its immediate right. The two pins that are toward the outside edge (the left) are to be connected to ground. The two pins on the right side toward the middle of the board are to be connected to +5 volts. The wiring is that simple. The LaserJet I/O power supply connector is plug compatible with the LaserWriter board. Because a power supply must be added to the NEC engine, the connector must be purchased as a separate item. One source is Don Thompson (see Sources). The pins should be soldered to the wires in the same manner as the interface cable pins were assembled to the cable. The wires then are inserted into the shell until they are fully locked into place. If the pins are not correctly inserted, the power to the board might be intermittent due to poor contact.

Again, whichever power supply is chosen for the NEC engine, AC should be drawn from the unused taps inside the power supply module. Remember the printer tour? The line can be run from the lugs using female disconnects which have been soldered to zip cord. One possible path for the cord to an external supply is shown in Fig. 5-2. The AC tap cord is then attached to the input screw terminals of the power supply, so that throwing the main printer switch also sends power to the logic board. If a small enough power supply has been chosen, it can be located inside the pedestal. Be aware, however, that the draw upon the supply is likely to produce considerable heat, which can damage both the supply and the printer if not properly dissipated. Make certain the printer's internal fan can cool the supply that has been chosen in the location selected. Mounting the supply externally allows cooling by convection.

Chapter 6

Serial cabling

Connecting the printer to the host computer, usually a Macintosh or IBM compatible, is one of those chores that ought to be easy and quick, but instead is fraught with lurking traps for the trusting and the light-hearted computer user. Nothing about computer cables is ever as simple as it should be.

The serial interface is supposed to be a standard across all types and brands of devices that use its protocol (Table 6-1), but that is not the case. Serial communication is a haphazard business. Some lines are used and others ignored. Some lines are crossed for no apparent reason, while others are shorted for equally invisible motives. I suspect the RS-232 "standard" was invented by a sadist and was gleefully accepted by all the masochists in computer design labs. (I argue that this standard is what the founding fathers had in mind when they proscribed "cruel and unusual punishment.")

Table 6-1. RS-232C DB-25 pin function assignments.

Pin	Input/output direction (DTE)	Assigned function
1		Frame ground (FG)
2	Out	Transmitted data (TXD)
3	In	Received data (RXD)
4	Out	Request to send (RTS)
5	In	Clear to send (CTS)
6	In	Data set ready (DSR)
7		Signal ground (SG)
8	In	Data carrier detect (DCD)
20	Out	Data terminal ready (DTR)

That things sometimes are transmitted successfully between machines is a wonder. Hardly two machines have the same signals assigned to the same lines. Still, if the lines of both machines are known, all is not lost: Usually something can be rigged to make the connection possible. Of course, that can be a very big "if." Some computer companies are strangely reticent about making such minor but critical disclosures to their patrons. Maybe they want to be the sole source of the cables, and maybe they do not want to frighten away the technology-shy buyer by cluttering up the user's manuals with assumedly intimidating schematics and tables. (Some persons actually find tables and schematics reassuring, but, then, there is no accounting for taste.) Whatever the reason, it does not make life easier for the person who has to connect two dissimilar devices in a serial network. The LaserWriter serial connections can be as difficult or as simple as you like, if you have the luck and perseverance to dig out the correct information.

Serial printer cables

Analog voltages are used to represent digital information in serial communication. With the RS-232C, the logical 1 is sent by forcing the voltage to -5 volts, while logical 0 is sent by switching the voltage to $+5$ volts. With other serial protocols, matched pairs of positive and negative lines, designated Transmitted Data Plus (TXD$+$), Transmitted Data Minus (TXD$-$), and their complements, Received Data Plus (RXD$+$) and Received Data Minus (RXD$-$), carry $+5$ volts and -5 volts respectively to represent serial logic. When the sender's TXD$+$ goes high (or low), its mated TXD$-$ goes (low) or high, and the receiver's RXD$+$ and RXD$-$ lines detect the difference between the incoming voltages and interpret a binary 1 (or 0), as the case might be.

The serial cable that is used to connect the host device to the LaserWriter is, therefore, very much machine specific. Different computers, even different computers from the same manufacturer, can require cables of very different wiring configurations. To attempt to cover every conceivable (or inconceivable) variation on the theme would exhaust both you as the reader and me as the writer. Therefore, such an attempt is not made. Only the most likely combinations are illustrated, those that with any luck will work in most, though not all, cases. There are always some oddball wiring schemes that only a lot of patience, in the absence of technical data, can untangle. The Gordian Knot of serial communications has yet to find its Alexander to resolve with one stroke all its complications.

Table 6-1 shows the conventional pin assignments for the RS-232C as used on data terminal equipment, i.e., the computer. The Input/Output direction would be reversed for data communications equipment, i.e., the printer. The functions should be self-evident.

If the machine is an IBM PS/2, then you will find a DB-9 connector, not a DB-25. Of course, the line signals are not the same, pin for pin, as in the DB-25 (Table 6-2).

Table 6-2. RS-232C DB-9 pin function assignments.

Pin	Input/output direction (DTE)	Assigned function
1	In	Data carrier detect (DCD)
2	In	Received data (RXD)
3	Out	Transmitted data (TXD)
4	Out	Data terminal ready (DTR)
5		Signal ground (SG)
6	In	Data set ready (DSR)
7	Out	Request to send (RTS)
8	In	Clear to send (CTS)

Yet another exquisite turn of the screw, however, is that another serial communications interface convention called the RS-422 exists. The RS-422 convention has been used in the Macintosh and the LaserWriter, and the DB-9 is also the avatar of its embodiment. (See Table 6-4 in section on Macintosh serial cables.)

IBM PC serial cables

By number, the IBM PC and PC clones take the first place for consideration. Short of adding a separate AppleTalk board to your computer (available for about $150), serial interfacing is the only game in town if a LaserWriter is to be the other player.

The parallel port of the PC is the default site of printer connection in the MS-DOS sphere of influence, but, as the LaserWriter was thoughtfully spared the embarrassment of being born with such an interface, it is very nearly impossible to use the parallel port to communicate with a LaserWriter. It has been possible for some years to interpose between a serial device and a parallel port a translator possessing the logic and digital hardware with which a stream of data, originating at the parallel port, can be massaged into a form useable by the serial device, but these ''smart'' cables are not always reliable, and the problem of setting their translation parameters is often intractable to all but the brute force method of solution.

These days, almost all PCs have at least one serial port, Com1:, built into their motherboards. Even those few that do not can be provided with one or more very cheaply and quickly by plugging in a serial or multifunction board.

Assuming, then, that the port exists, it is usually of the DB-25 type in the PC/PC-XT. In the newer PC-AT and PS/2 computers, it is usually the DB-9. The computer might have either a male or female connector, but the LaserWriter is by Apple's fiat given a female DB-25 and a female DB-9. Therefore, depending upon your computer, the cable to be constructed will require one male DB-25 or DB-9 for the LaserWriter's end of the cable and either a male or female DB-25 or DB-9 for the computer's.

The most frequently found wiring scheme for DB-25 to DB-25 printer interfacing is that in which the transmit and receive data lines are crossed: Line 2 on the sending end of the cable terminates on pin 3 of the receiving end, and line 3 of the sender is crossed to pin 2 of the receiver. By using just these two lines (Table 6-3), interfacing can be accomplished in many, if not most, cases. If the computer uses the DB-9 connector, the line pairings will be line 3 (TXD) of the DB-9 to line 3 (RXD) of the DB-25 and the computer's line 2 (RXD) to the printer's DB-25 line 2 (TXD).

If the composite interface has been built, then again, two lines will usually serve to make the connection. In the case of the DB-25, line 2 of the sending computer should terminate on pin 9 at the LaserWriter end of the cable, and line 3 from the computer ends at pin 5 of the LaserWriter DB-9. From the DB-9 RS-232 to LaserWriter DB-9 RS-422 (AppleTalk) port, the wiring is as follows: Line 3 of the computer to line 9 of the LaserWriter, and line 2 of the computer to line 5 of the

Table 6-3. Simple PC serial interface cables.

Computer DB-25	LaserWriter DB-25	Computer DB-9	LaserWriter DB-25
Line 2	Line 3	Line 2	Line 2
Line 3	Line 2	Line 3	Line 3

Computer DB-25	LaserWriter DB-9	Computer DB-9	LaserWriter DB-9
Line 2	Line 9	Line 2	Line 5
Line 3	Line 5	Line 3	Line 9

Table 6-4. RS-422 DB-9 pin function assignments.

Pin	Input/output direction (DTE)	Assigned function
1		Frame ground (FG)
2	Out	+5 volts
3		Signal ground (SG)
4	Out	Transmit data plus (TXD+)
5	Out	Transmit data minus (TXD−)
6	Out	+12 volts
7	In	Handshake (HSK)
8	In	Receive data plus (RXD+)
9	In	Receive data minus (RXD−)

printer. (Wiring diagrams for these cables and others in this chapter appear in Appendix D.)

The IBM DB-25 cable wiring applies equally to Apple II, Atari ST, and Amiga computers, as well as to the PC and PC clones.

Macintosh serial cables

As mentioned, Macintosh serial connection adds a further dimension in confusion. The original Macintoshes (128K, 512K, 512KE) use the DB-9 RS-422, (for pin outs, see Table 6-4), while Macintoshes of more recent manufacture (Plus, SE series, II series) use the mini DIN-8 RS-423 connector (Table 6-5 and Fig. 6-1).

The Apple IIGS, an amalgam of Apple II and Mac technologies, also uses the mini DIN-8, and it has borrowed the Mac's ROM-based hardware support for Apple-Talk. The Mac XL and Lisa 2 use the same DB-25 connector and connections as the IBM PC, Atari ST, and Amiga, although the port is RS-422/AppleTalk capable.

A simple Macintosh serial cable conforms to the same principles as does the PC cable. Crossing the transmit and receive data lines between the computer and the printer accomplishes the link. Therefore, from Table 6-4, the Mac's DB-9 connections are as follows: Pin 5 of the Mac to pin 3 of the DB-25 of the printer and pin 9 of

Table 6-5. Mac RS-423 DIN 8 pin function assignments.

Pin	Input/output direction	Assigned function
1	In	Data terminal ready (DTR)
2	Out	Data set ready (DSR)
3	Out	Transmit data minus (TXD –)
4		Signal ground (SG)
5	In	Receive data minus (RXD –)
6	Out	Transmit data plus (TXD +)
7	Out	Data carrier detect (DCD)
8	In	Receive data plus (RXD +)

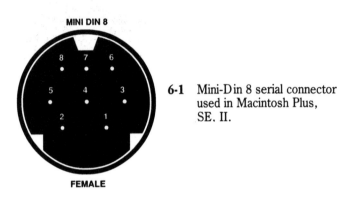

6-1 Mini-Din 8 serial connector used in Macintosh Plus, SE, II.

the Mac to pin 2 of the printer. To connect to the printer's DB-9 AppleTalk port, merely cross lines 5 and 9 of each connector, so that line 5 of the Mac goes to line 9 of the LaserWriter, and line 9 of the Mac to line 5 of the LaserWriter. In the newer Macintoshes, the pin out plan for the mini DIN-8 connector is shown in Table 6-5 and in the accompanying diagram in Fig. 6-1.

When called upon to connect devices using different serial protocols, you must find the lowest common denominator that permits the establishment of the link. Thus, if an RS-232 port is to talk to an RS-422/423 port, the negative pins only of the RS-422/423 are used to send and receive data, while the RXD + is grounded and the TXD + remains unconnected. In the case of the Macintosh to the LaserWriter, however, it is possible to fall back upon the two-line method, disregarding the positive lines because the Mac's serial interface chip reverts to simple RS-232 protocol if called upon to do so. From pin 3 of the mini DIN-8, connect to pin 3 of the DB-25 or pin 9 of the DB-9 of the LaserWriter, and from pin 5 of the mini DIN-8 connect to pin 2 of the LaserWriter DB-25 or to pin 5 of its DB-9.

Table 6-6 shows simple Macintosh to LaserWriter serial cables and is included for those who, for whatever reason, wish to bypass AppleTalk. Remember, however, that failure to use AppleTalk can jeopardize each node of the network, that is, both the Macintosh and the LaserWriter.

Table 6-6. Simple Mac serial cables.

Mac DB-25	LaserWriter DB-25	Mac DB-25	LaserWriter DB-9
Pin 2	Pin 3	Pin 2	Pin 9
Pin 3	Pin 2	Pin 3	Pin 5

Mac DB-9	LaserWriter DB-25	Mac DB-9	LaserWriter DB-9
Pin 5	Pin 3	Pin 5	Pin 9
Pin 9	Pin 2	Pin 9	Pin 5

Mac Mini-Din 8	LaserWriter DB-25	Mac Mini-Din 8	LaserWriter DB-9
Pin 3	Pin 3	Pin 3	Pin 9
Pin 5	Pin 2	Pin 5	Pin 5

Handshaking

Sometimes it is necessary to provide other signals to the serial interface of the computer in order for communication to take place. This is a form of *handshaking*, and the number of forms that serial handshaking can assume would do justice to any secret society. And then, the difference between hardware and software handshaking must be considered. In general, Apple has solved the question of handshaking by ignoring it: Apple to Apple communication entirely avoids hardware handshaking, and this introduces some problems for persons who wish to connect their computers to Apple products such as the LaserWriter.

Hardware handshaking

The crossing of the data transmit and data receive lines sets the pattern for full handshaking, wherein all the paired lines in use are crossed to their complements. Thus, the request-to-send line is crossed with the clear-to-send line, and the data-set-ready line is crossed with the data-terminal-ready line.

For the computer RS-232 DB-25 to LaserWriter DB-25 cable (Table 6-7), the lines are matched as follows: Pin 2 of the computer to pin 3 of the LaserWriter, pin 3 of the computer to pin 2 of the LaserWriter, pin 4 of the computer to pin 5 of the LaserWriter, pin 5 of the computer to pin 4 of the LaserWriter, pin 6 of the computer to pin 20 of the LaserWriter, and pin 20 of the computer to pin 6 of the LaserWriter. The signal ground and data carrier detect lines of each end are connected straight

Table 6-7. PC RS-232 DB-25 to LaserWriter DB-25.

Signal	TXD	RXD	RTS	CTS	DSR	SG	DCD	DTR
PC DB-25	Pin 2	Pin 3	Pin 4	Pin 5	Pin 6	Pin 7	Pin 8	Pin 20
LW DB-25	Pin 3	Pin 2	Pin 5	Pin 4	Pin 20	Pin 7	Pin 8	Pin 6
Signal	RXD	TXD	CTS	RTS	DTR	SG	DCD	DSR

through. This means that the number 7 pins (SG) on each end are matched, as are the two pins in position 8 (DCD) of each connector.

For the RS-232 DB-9 to LaserWriter DB-25 (Table 6-8), the pins are paired so that pin 2 of the computer goes to pin 2 of the printer, pin 3 of the computer goes to pin 3 of the printer, pin 4 of the computer goes to pin 6 of the printer, pin 6 of the computer goes to pin 20 of the printer, pin 7 of the computer goes to pin 5 of the printer, and pin 8 of the computer goes to pin 4 of the printer. Again, SG and DCD are paired straight through: Line 5 (SG) of the computer to line 7 of the printer, and line 1 (DCD) of the computer to line 8 of the LaserWriter.

Table 6-8. PC RS-232 DB-9 to LaserWriter DB-25.

Signal	DCD	RXD	TXD	DTR	SG	DSR	RTS	CTS
PC DB-9	Pin 1	Pin 2	Pin 3	Pin 4	Pin 5	Pin 6	Pin 7	Pin 8
LW DB-25	Pin 8	Pin 2	Pin 3	Pin 6	Pin 7	Pin 20	Pin 5	Pin 4
Signal	DCD	TXD	RXD	DSR	SG	DTR	CTS	RTS

Either one of these configurations can be called a *null modem condition*, although there are other candidates for that nomination.

In cases where the preceding handshaking configurations do not work, some variations might, with luck, provide a workable alternative. These involve shorting the RTS and CTS lines to each other at both ends of the cable; that is, in the DB-25 to DB-25 cable (Table 6-9), lines 4 and 5 at each end are connected to one another within the connector housing and do not pass through to the opposite end. Similarly, in the PC DB-9 to LW DB-25 cable (Table 6-10), the 7 and 8 pins of the DB-9 are connected to one another, while at the LaserWriter's end of the cable, pins 4 and 5 of the DB-25 are connected. Note that these shorted connections are to be made in the cable that connects the computer to the printer, not within the devices themselves.

Table 6-9. PC RS-232 DB-25 to LaserWriter DB-25: Handshaking.

Signal	TXD	RXD	RTS = CTS	DSR	SG	DCD	DTR
PC DB-25	Pin 2	Pin 3	Pin 4 = Pin 5	Pin 6	Pin 7	Pin 8	Pin 20
LW DB-25	Pin 3	Pin 2	Pin 5 = Pin 4	Pin 20	Pin 7	Pin 8	Pin 6
Signal	RXD	TXD	CTS = RTS	DTR	SG	DCD	DSR

Table 6-10. PC RS-232 DB-9 to LaserWriter DB-25: Handshaking.

Signal	DCD	RXD	TXD	DTR	SG	DSR	RTS = CTS
PC DB-9	Pin 1	Pin 2	Pin 3	Pin 4	Pin 5	Pin 6	Pin 7 = Pin 8
LW DB-25	Pin 8	Pin 2	Pin 3	Pin 6	Pin 7	Pin 20	Pin 5 = Pin 4
Signal	DCD	TXD	RXD	DSR	SG	DTR	CTS = RTS

Should these arrangements fail to satisfy the handshaking requirements of the computer, additional lines must be shorted, beginning with the DSR to DTR at both ends. Thus, in the DB-25 to DB-25 (Table 6-11), lines 6 and 20 are connected to each other. In the PC DB-9 to LW DB-25 (Table 6-12), lines 6 and 4 of the DB-9 are interconnected and, again, at the DB-25, lines 6 and 20 are shorted.

Table 6-11. PC RS-232 DB-25 to LaserWriter DB-25: Handshaking.

Signal	TXD	RXD	RTS = CTS	DSR = DTR	SG	DCD
PC DB-25	Pin 2	Pin 3	Pin 4 = Pin 5	Pin 6 = Pin 20	Pin 7	Pin 8
LW DB-25	Pin3	Pin 2	Pin 5 = Pin 4	Pin 20 = Pin 6	Pin7	Pin 8
Signal	RXD	TXD	CTS = RTS	DTR = DSR	SG	DCD

Table 6-12. PC RS-232 DB-9 to LaserWriter DB-25: Handshaking.

Signal	DCD	RXD	TXD	DTR = DSR	RTS = CTS	SG
PC DB-9	Pin 1	Pin 2	Pin 3	Pin 4 = Pin 6	Pin 7 = Pin 8	Pin 5
LW DB-25	Pin 8	Pin 2	Pin 3	Pin 6 = Pin 20	Pin 5 = Pin 4	Pin 7
Signal	DCD	TXD	RXD	DSR = DTR	CTS = RTS	SG

In the event that these methods also fail, then shorting the DCD line to the DSR and DTR lines might succeed in providing the requisite signals. Therefore, as a last resort, in the DB-25 to DB-25 cable (Table 6-13), short lines 6, 8, and 20 together at both ends of the cable. In the DB-9 to DB-25 cable (Table 6-14), short lines 4, 6, and 1 together at the DB-9 end and lines 6, 8, and 20 at the DB-25. Note that this configuration is in addition to the shorting of the RTS and CTS lines, and, for perversity's sake, is sometimes called a *null modem*.

Table 6-13. PC RS-232 DB-25 to LaserWriter DB-25: Null handshaking.

Signal	TXD	RXD	RTS = CTS	DSR = DCD = DTR	SG
PC DB-25	Pin 2	Pin 3	Pin 4 = Pin 5	Pin 6 = Pin 8 = Pin 20	Pin 7
LW DB-25	Pin 3	Pin 2	Pin 5 = Pin 4	Pin 20 = Pin 8 = Pin 6	Pin 7
Signal	RXD	TXD	CTS = RTS	DTR = DCD = DSR	SG

Table 6-14. PC RS-232 DB-9 to LaserWriter DB-25: Null handshaking.

Signal	RXD	TXD	DCD = DTR = DSR	RTS = CTS	SG
PC DB-9	Pin 2	Pin 3	Pin 1 = Pin 4 = Pin 6	Pin 7 = Pin 8	Pin 5
LW DB-25	Pin 2	Pin 3	Pin 8 = Pin 6 = Pin 20	Pin 5 = Pin 4	Pin 7
Signal	TXD	RXD	DCD = DSR = DTR	CTS = RTS	SG

A variant that excludes the shorting of the RTS and CTS lines but that demands the shorting of the others does exist. For good measure, this condition is sometimes termed *full handshaking*. Such a cable (Tables 6-15, 6-16) crosses the RTS and CTS lines through to either end of the cable, but shorts the DSR, DTR, and DCD within each end.

Table 6-15. PC RS-232 DB-25 to LaserWriter DB-25: Full handshaking.

Signal	TXD	RXD	RTS = CTS	DSR = DCD = DTR	SG
PC DB-25	Pin 2	Pin 3	Pin 4 = Pin 5	Pin 6 = Pin 8 = Pin 20	Pin 7
LW DB-25	Pin 3	Pin 2	Pin 5 = Pin 4	Pin 20 = Pin 8 = Pin 6	Pin 7
Signal	RXD	TXD	CTS = RTS	DTR = DCD = DSR	SG

Table 6-16. PC RS-232 DB-9 to LaserWriter DB-25: Full handshaking.

Signal	RXD	TXD	DCD = DTR = DSR	RTS	CTS	SG
PC DB-9	Pin 2	Pin 3	Pin 1 = Pin 4 = Pin 6	Pin 7	Pin 8	Pin 5
LW DB-25	Pin 2	Pin 3	Pin 8 = Pin 6 = Pin 20	Pin 5	Pin 4	Pin 7
Signal	TXD	RXD	DCD = DSR = DTR	CTS	RTS	SG

What some people are pleased to call a *no handshake* connection is obtained by shorting the CTS, DSR, DTR, and DCD lines, while leaving the RTS lines out of the picture altogether. Thus, lines 5, 6, 8, and 20 are shorted together at both ends of the DB-25 to DB-25 cable (Table 6-17), leaving line 4 entirely unconnected, or floating, while, in the DB-9 to DB-25 cable (Table 6-18), lines 1, 4, 6, and 8 are shorted in the DB-9 and lines 5, 6, 8, and 20 are shorted at the DB-25 end.

Table 6-17. PC RS-232 DB-25 to LaserWriter DB-25: No handshaking.

Signal	TXD	RXD	RTS	SG	CTS = DSR = DCD = DTR
PC DB-25	Pin 2	Pin 3	Pin 4 UC	Pin 7	Pin 5 = Pin 6 = Pin 8 = Pin 20
LW DB-25	Pin 3	Pin 2	Pin 4 UC	Pin 7	Pin 5 = Pin 20 = Pin 8 = Pin 6
Signal	RXD	TXD	RTS	SG	CTS = DTR = DCD = DSR

Table 6-18. PC RS-232 DB-9 to LaserWriter DB-25: No handshaking.

Signal	RXD	TXD	DCD = DTR = DSR = CTS	RTS	SG
PC DB-9	Pin 2	Pin 3	Pin 1 = Pin 4 = Pin 6 = Pin 8	Pin 7 UC	Pin 5
LW DB-25	Pin 2	Pin 3	Pin 8 = Pin 6 = Pin 20 = Pin 5	Pin 4 UC	Pin 7
Signal	TXD	RXD	DCD = DSR = DTR = CTS	RTS	SG

If you connect some PCs or PC clones to the LaserWriter through the LaserWriter's RS-422/AppleTalk DB-9 port, and, if the host computer is one of those that demands handshaking, complications begin to set in almost immediately. In general, first attempt to establish communication using one of the simple cables described in the preceding paragraphs. If that should fail, then try one of the combinations in the following paragraphs. (See the schemata figures in Appendix B.)

In the PC DB-25 to LW DB-9 connection, short the RTS, CTS, DCD, DSR, and DTR lines (4, 5, 6, 8, 20 respectively) at the DB-25 end, while lines 1 and 8 (GND, RXD+) of the DB-9 are shorted at the DB-9. In addition, line 7 (SG) of the DB-25 should pass through to line 1 of the DB-9, making a 3-way connection at the LW end of the cable. The TXD and RXD lines are crossed, with line 2 of the DB-25 connected to line 9 of the DB-9 and line 3 of the DB-25 connected to line 5 of the DB-9.

In the PC RS-232 DB-9 to LW RS-422 DB-9 connection, short together pins 1, 4, 6, 7, and 8 of the PC cable end connector and pins 1 and 8 at the LW cable end. Line 5 of the PC should also be tied to line 1 of the LW, providing a reference. Cross the TXD and RXD lines so that 2 of the PC goes to 5 of the LW, and 3 of the PC goes to 9 of the LW.

If any of these configurations are to be attempted, it is sensible to purchase or to construct a serial jumper box so that the potential combinations can be tried before actually hard wiring the finished cable. A jumper box consists of two DB connector shells mounted to a perforated block of isolated conductors, allowing temporary connection of any lines by means of short lengths of wire which plug into the block between the connectors. Thus, any custom scheme can be tested and proved or rejected before resorting to solder.

In all cases, first attempt the simple two line cable as suggested in the previous section. You should not subject yourself to the perils of hardware handshaking unless it is unavoidable.

Ready made

For those disinclined to build a cable, in the great majority of instances, pre-wired cables can be purchased to fill the need. Look for a printer cable, null modem cable, or modem eliminator cable with the appropriate connectors. Of course, as has been seen, these terms have arbitrary attributes, and two cables with the same name can represent wholly incompatible wiring schemes. Unless you know precisely what the host computer requires for handshaking, an expensive collection of pre-wired cables can be accumulated as various options are tried and found to be wanting. Therefore, if at all possible, never buy a cable without first determining the handshaking of the computer, either from its technical manuals or from its manufacturer (dealers or mail order vendors seldom know these things) and inquiring just what the seller of the cable means by, for instance, ''null modem.'' For software handshaking solutions, consult the section on communications software.

Chapter 7

AppleTalk
computer
cabling

The connection for Appletalk ("The Rest of Us") would appear to require a rather short chapter, because Apple's decision to build networking hardware and firmware into their machines limits the ways in which you can err. However, as was seen in the section devoted to power supplies, there are worms in the Apple even here.

Apple AppleTalk

Apple sells connectors for all of the machines that it still supports. The AppleTalk package contains the port adaptor, which co-opts the serial printer port and terminates in the AppleTalk box, an extension cable for adding length between two cables, and a female to female splicing adaptor to mate two extension cables. The cables simply plug in to the appropriate ports of the various nodes, and the network is effectively created. The cost of each node is $75.

Mixing AppleTalk with OtherTalk

Whenever Apple creates a product that it sells for about five times its real value, it also creates a market for third-party vendors who are content to sell the same product for only twice its worth. AppleTalk is no exception: indeed, it is exemplary. At any rate, you do have cheaper alternatives to the party line.

Farrallon's PhoneNet and ARC's Modunet use telephone or twisted pair wiring to replace AppleTalk. Each can be integrated with an existing AppleTalk network, and each costs less than half of Apple's price per node. The added advantages of PhoneNet, for instance, include increased electrical isolation of each node, the ability to use existing phone lines, and the ability to use the same telephone wiring for simultaneous analog voice or data transmission and digital computer networking.

Even more inexpensive are the AppleTalk clone connectors sold by Jameco and others. These clone connectors are electrically identical to, and can be substituted for, AppleTalk hardware. They pass the duck test (Fig. 7-1).

YourOwnNet

If you could find out exactly what was used in constructing an AppleTalk network connector, you could then become a clone builder yourself. Not surprisingly, Don Lancaster has published the components list and a schematic for AppleTalk "cheater" cables. (See his article "Ask The Guru" in the December 1987 *Computer Shopper* on page 147 and in the January 1988 *ATG* on page 265.)

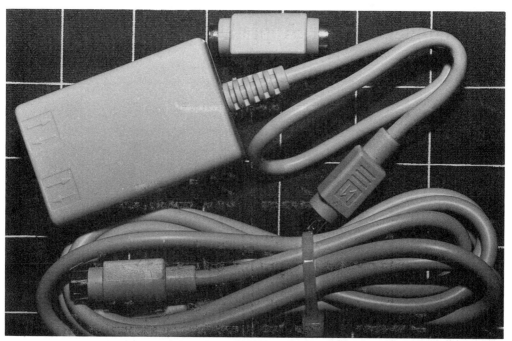

7-1 A clone AppleTalk connector.

Internally (Fig. 7-2), the AppleTalk cable is a connector that attaches the five AppleTalk lines (GND, RXD –, TXD –, RXD +, and TXD +) to the primary windings of a small iron core coil (containing, according to Lancaster, two primary windings of 35 turns and a secondary of 70 turns), with 1K resistors interposed between the transformer and the RXD plus and minus lines. The TXD lines go directly to the primaries, along with the resistor terminated lines. One side of the secondary is connected to ground through a bypass composed of a 0.1μF capacitor, a 1K resistor, a 1 Megohm resistor, and a 100 ohm resistor connected to a single pole double throw switch in the AppleTalk mini-DIN connectors. The other side of the secondary is connected to the other two pins of the 3 pin mini-DIN connectors that feed into shielded 78 ohm cables. (The switch is closed if one mini-DIN connector is unused.)

It is also possible, again according to Lancaster, to use simple bell or telephone wire to make an AppleTalk substitute cable. Lines run straight between the TXD – and TXD + pins of each node's connector, with leads branching off those direct lines to the respective RXD minus and plus pins. Place 1K ohm resistors in each of the branch lines serving the RXD pins. One additional line is provided for the ground. Lancaster claims that this form of pseudo-AppleTalk is safe, if all the nodes are plugged into the same grounded AC outlet. This seems to be both less risky than the direct-connect wiring while being less safe than the AppleTalk hardware.

The direct connect method works. It is simple. It is fast. And, as has been recounted in the section devoted to Overpowering, it is fraught with peril. However, for those willing to take the chance, or in a real emergency when connectors are not available, the connections are listed in Table 7-1. Again, observe suitable grounding precautions. *Use at your own risk.*

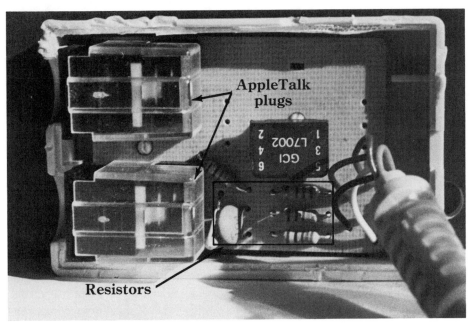

7-2   Inside an AppleTalk (LocalTalk) connector.

Table 7-1. AppleTalk (LocalTalk) direct-connect cables.

Machine Connector type	Mac XL/Lisa 2 DB-25	Mac 128, 512 DB-9	MacPlus, SE, II DIN-8	LW/LW Plus DB-9
Read pin assignments across table	pin 20 ⇒ LW	pin 4	pin 6	Mac ⇐ pin 8
	pin 2 ⇒ LW	pin 5	pin 3	Mac ⇐ pin 9
	pin 9 ⇒ LW	pin 8	pin 8	Mac ⇐ pin 4
	pin 3 ⇒ LW	pin 9	pin 5	Mac ⇐ pin 5

Chapter 8

Computer to printer communication

Having provided your computer and printer with an appropriate cable, it remains only to set the software parameters that the computer and printer will use for data transmission. The Macintosh has the easiest time of it here once again, since the Mac and the LaserWriter are meant to work transparently one with the other through AppleTalk (LocalTalk).

The IBM world can also enjoy the ease of connection which AppleTalk makes possible, providing that an AppleTalk board has been installed in the PC, but, for the purposes of this discussion, this option is not considered, because most PC to LaserWriter connections are of the simple serial type, and most PC software that supports PostScript assumes this type of connection.

Macintosh AppleTalk

Once the connectors have been plugged together and both the printer and computer are up and running, the time has arrived to let the Macintosh operating system know that a LaserWriter is available for printing. Two files need to be added to the System Folder (System 6.0x and lower) on the startup disk, whether it be a micro-floppy or hard drive, LaserWriter or Laser Prep. The LaserWriter Driver is a program that contains the necessary handshaking and data transfer information for the Macintosh to operate a LaserWriter, and Laser Prep is a file of Apple-defined PostScript extensions that is automatically downloaded to the printer the first time that the LaserWriter is used each printing session. Laser Prep resides in the LaserWriter RAM for as long as the printer is turned on, and is loaded at the beginning of the first print job only. If the printer is turned off and then on again, or a reset occurs, then the file is downloaded again, otherwise its presence is unnoticeable to the user.

Also, the Desk Accessory Chooser must be available under the Apple menu. (See your Owner's Manual for the use of DAs and Font/DA mover.)

Assuming that Chooser is present (it is if you have used any type of printer with your Mac), then simply place the LaserWriter and Laser Prep files in your System folder of your hard drive or in each System folder of every micro-floppy that you will be using as a startup disk. (See the Owner's Manual for dragging file icons and copying files.) Then select Chooser from the Apple menu. You will be presented with a window (Fig. 8-1) with three boxes.

The left-hand box will contain icons for all of the printer drivers in the active System folder. The LaserWriter icon should be visible. (If it is not, then check the System folder to make certain that the file is there. If it is, try resetting the computer by tapping the programmer's switch.) Using the mouse, select the LaserWriter icon. This will activate the radio buttons at the bottom of the Chooser window. Select the top button (Active). This will bring up a dialog box telling you that Apple-Talk requires the presence of an AppleTalk network and connectors. (If you get a dialog box saying that the printer port is busy, then it will be necessary to reset the

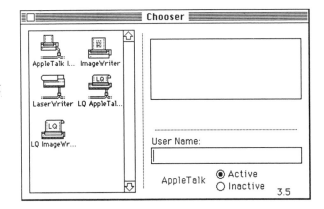

8-1 Macintosh Chooser desk accessory, showing Printer and Network icons for device drivers available.

computer before proceeding in order to clear the port for AppleTalk.) Click the OK button, and look in the top right-hand box. If the computer has recognized the presence of a LaserWriter on the network, then the name of the printer (LaserWriter, LaserWriter Plus) will appear highlighted in the window (Fig. 8-2). If the name is there, then you have successfully created a LocalTalk network, and the LaserWriter will be ready to print from any application which supports printing. You will need to install the screen bit-map fonts into your System for each of the typefaces in your LaserWriter, if you intend to take advantage of the printer's built-in typeface families, but henceforth, all that you need to do in order to print a document is to select Print from the application's File menu as you normally would for any other printer.

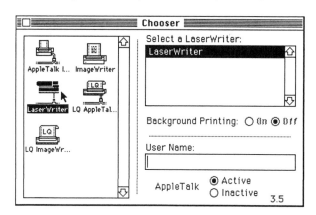

8-2 Macintosh Chooser desk accessory, showing result of selection of LaserWriter icon. The highlighted name shows that the LaserWriter is powered on and available for printing.

If the LaserWriter name does not appear in the top right-hand box of the Chooser window, then the LaserWriter cannot be found. Click the bottom radio button (Inactive), and you will be presented with a dialog box reminding you to disconnect the AppleTalk connector from the printer port. Click OK. Close Chooser, check the connections of the AppleTalk cabling, both at the printer and at the computer, and check that the two cables are properly mated to each other. Then select Chooser again from the Apple menu. Again, select the LaserWriter icon and click on the Active radio button. If the LaserWriter name still does not appear in the upper right-hand box, then it is time to restart the entire system, both computer and printer and try again.

Usually, a loose connection is the cause of most problems in getting a LaserWriter recognized on the network, so double and triple check each of the cable connections. If nothing seems to work, then it might be that one or both of the AppleTalk cables is defective. (If you are using the direct connect cable method, then break down and get proper AppleTalk cables. This will probably solve the problem.) If the cables are functioning, then either the computer or printer requires service.

In all likelihood, you will have no problems in getting the LaserWriter on line. It helps to leave the LaserWriter end of the AppleTalk cable unplugged when the printer is going through its warm-up cycle. Plugging in the cable before applying power can prevent the printing of a test page after powering on the printer. Wait until the yellow light has started to flash or until the test page has been ejected before connecting the cable to the printer.

Serial communications

The serial communication mode is for the ''rest of you.'' On the typical IBM PC or PC clone, the printer is connected to the Com1: serial port. It is necessary to set the parameters at which that port is to operate in order for the printer to be able to receive data for printing and for the computer to receive messages from the printer.

The simplest way to send a PostScript file to the LaserWriter from an MS-DOS machine is simply to copy the file's contents to the serial port. This is done from the command line MS-DOS shell. The procedure requires that the MODE command be used to set the port's parameters to match those of the LaserWriter. Assuming that the LaserWriter is operating at 9600 baud, the command would be as follows:

```
MODE com1: 9600,N,8,1
```

This translates to 9600 baud, No parity, 8 data bits per data word (7 can be specified instead), and 1 stop bit, all of which are acceptable to the LaserWriter.

The file is then dumped to the port by the COPY command, as in:

```
COPY FILE.PS COM1:
```

This command tells the operating system to send a copy of the file FILE.PS to the serial port. The original file is left untouched, while the copy is directed to the printer attached to the port, where it is interpreted and printed. This method works for small files that have been thoroughly debugged. The file must be short and error free, because of the smallness of the input buffer in the LaserWriter's RAM, the inability of the printer to request a pause in the transmission, and the failure to provide for error reporting. Be aware, also, that the serial port parameters remain as set only for as long as the computer remains on or until they are changed by other software. To set the parameters automatically at start-up, add the MODE statement to the autoexec.bat file.

A better method of communication is through one of the standard terminal emulation programs for the PC, such as ProComm or SuperComm. These establish a two-way communications mode with the printer, so that there is an interactive relationship between the user and the PostScript interpreter. The parameters remain the same for baud rate, parity, data bits, and stop bits, but it is almost mandatory that the software handshaking protocol XON/XOFF be invoked as well in order that long files can be safely uploaded to the printer without buffer overflow or data loss.

If the program that you intend to use does not provide XON/XOFF handshaking, then find one that does. The printer can be set for hardware handshaking, involving construction of one of the exasperating cable configurations from the previous chapter, but it is not a recommended practice, because, in addition to the annoyance attendant to the fabrication of the correct cable, you must alter the contents of the LaserWriter's EEPROM (*electrically erasable programmable read only memory*). The EEPROM can be written to a total of 5000 times during the life of the logic board, after which it is rendered inoperable. Writing to the EEPROM should be done only with forethought and under compulsion of necessity.

Remember, because you have purchased a used board, the number of times that the EEPROM had previously been addressed is an unknown variable. Diablo emulation, which is possible through a downloaded program, allows the setting of the daisy wheel character set, analogous to changing the daisy wheel of the 630 printer. Because this also uses the EEPROM and the former owner might have made frequent changes to this area of the chip, the risk in writing to the EEPROM becomes even greater. Do not make changes to the EEPROM without consideration of these perils (see Appendix A).

For normal terminal programs, full duplex can be used, although half duplex works if the first command sent to the printer is the PostScript EXECUTIVE command, which places the printer in its interactive mode and provides you with a PostScript prompt and echo of typed or uploaded input.

Chapter 9

Status indicator LEDs

The DC controller board provides three printer status indicator signals that can be tapped for an LED display (Fig. 9-1). These give the user information concerning the online, busy, and paper out conditions of the printer.

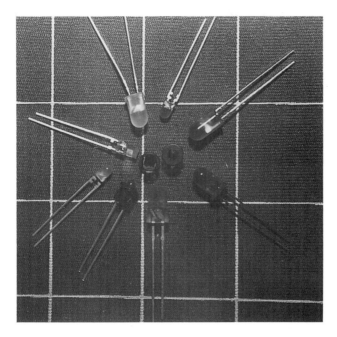

9-1 Assorted LEDs and LED mounts.

Typically, a green light is used to show that the printer is on, is warmed up, and is ready to receive data. This LED flashes during the warm-up cycle, which can last from 1 to 2 minutes, as the laser and fusion environments are warmed to operating temperatures. A steady green is shown when warm-up has been completed and throughout normal operation.

A yellow light is used to indicate the printer busy condition. This light begins flashing during the warm-up to indicate that the printer's logic board has begun to process the data from ROM that produces a test page when warm-up has been completed. The LaserWriter test page is illustrated in the Fig. 9-2. The yellow light also flashes during normal operation as data is received and processed by the printer's CPU and DC controller for printing. During printing, the yellow LED goes out but comes on again as the next page is processed.

A steady yellow lamp indicates the paper out condition of the paper cassette, or that the printer is waiting for paper to be fed manually. If the paper out condition persists longer than the permissible period, as defined by PostScript for the duration of a timeout, then a timeout error is registered and the current job is lost. If the paper out condition is resolved before a timeout error occurs, normal printing

9-2 LaserWriter test page. The middle of three overlapping representations of pages in center of the test page shows current LaserWriter communications protocol, in this case AppleTalk. Dog-eared page symbol at bottom shows number of pages registered in the page counter kept in the EEPROM of LaserWriter board.

resumes, with no data loss. An exception to this is the incoming-data-buffer overflow error, which can occur during a timeout if proper handshaking is not observed between the computer software and the printer. This condition is not shown by any of the status lights, and all printer functions appear to continue in the routine manner, but the result of an overflow error is the unannounced cessation of normal operation after the pages currently in memory have been printed. If, for instance, the overflow should occur during the printing of a multi-page document or during a print merge session, the yellow busy light flashes with deceptive assurance, but no pages are printed and all data sent subsequent to the error are lost. In such a case, it is necessary to halt the printing job (type Control – period on the Macintosh) and to start a new job, resuming at the next numerically ordered page in the interrupted sequence.

A red LED is used to indicate a paper jam. Normally, this light is out. A steady red light shows that a paper error has occurred, a condition that can range from a failure of the pick-up rollers of the cassette to a misalignment of the paper within the engine itself. The printer must be shut down and opened to clear a paper jam error, resulting in loss of the current job and forcing a cold restart of the printer.

Accessing the status signals

Signals for the three status LEDs are derived from the J-201 six-pin header at the right front corner of the DC controller board. (See Fig. 1-11 and Fig. 9-3.) Pin 1 is in the rearmost position, with pin 6 toward the front of the printer. Pins 1 through 4 are used for the display. Therefore, a straight four- or six-pin Molex connector is required to plug into J-201. A larger connector can be cut down, if one of the correct size cannot be obtained.

Power is drawn from pin 1. Pin 2 delivers the ready signal to a green LED. Run a line from Pin 1 to the anode (longer leg) of the green LED, and run the return from the second leg to pin two. A 150 ohm resistor should be placed between the LED's cathode and pin 2. The other LEDs are wired in the same fashion, the yellow busy LED being connected to power and pin 3, with the necessary 150 ohm resistor, and the red paper jam LED wired to pin 4, also with the same value resistor. (See Fig. 9-4 and the LED schematic in Appendix B.)

The LEDs can be mounted on a piece of scrap printed circuit board or on perf board. Three 1/4 inch holes drilled in the front of the lid and fitted with LED holders will receive the finished display (Fig. 9-5.) Allow enough length for the leads of the wiring harness from the display PC board to the DC controller so that the lid can be lifted to allow unplugging of the molex connector at J-201 should service be necessary.

9-3 Location of pins on DC controller board for status LED connections.

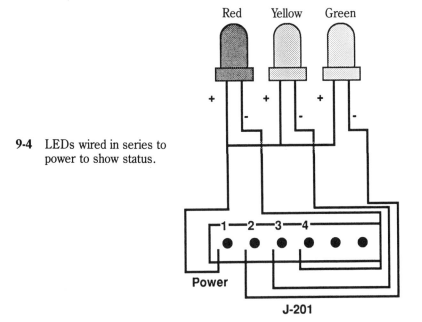

9-4 LEDs wired in series to power to show status.

9-5 Location for mounting LEDs in upper right front of lid bezel.

Chapter 10

Testing the assembled printer

With all of the connections made, it is time to see if anything works as expected. Load the toner cartridge through the flip-down door on the right-hand end of the printer. It fits just one way. The rotating pages-processed gauge should be visible through the window in the door. Insert the paper cassette with its load of paper. Attach the proper computer to printer cabling. If the switch has been built, set it for the appropriate communications mode as shown in the table in chapter 5. If no switch has been built, the printer will be using AppleTalk, like it or not. If the switch is present and the LED has been mounted as described, then turn on the power to the printer.

The fan motor should start and and the interface LED should briefly illuminate and then extinguish. The status display should then be given attention. If the green LED is flashing, then the laser engine is warming up. After about 30 – 45 seconds, the yellow LED should begin flashing at a slightly slower rate than the green LED. The yellow indicates that the LaserWriter logic board has awakened and is busy sensing the interface condition and preparing to print its start-up test page. After about 90 – 120 seconds, the main drive motor should then turn on and the sound of the paper pick-up mechanism should be heard as a page is fed from the cassette. The green LED should have become steady, and the yellow LED should be extinguished. The test page should then be ejected.

If the above series of events do not occur as described, turn the printer off, go read the *Hitchhiker's Guide to the Galaxy*, and, when the panic has subsided, check all of the connections twice before concluding that something is broken. A loose power connector is the most common fault found in any electrical device, so begin there.

Look first at the power connector on the logic board at J-7. Make certain that it is seated and that each header pin is in contact with the corresponding socket pin. The two innermost pins deliver the 5 volts to the board. After checking the power connector at the board end, also check the connections to the power supply itself, particularly if you have started with the NEC engine. Lastly, if you have added a power supply, remember that the logic board demands a full 5 volts, so check the voltage coming to the board with a voltmeter.

If all the power connections and voltages appear to be normal, then study the start-up sequence, paying particular attention to the green LED on the interface switch board. If it lighted and then extinguished at the time of powering on the printer, then it is likely that the logic board and your interface connections are as they should be. If it came on and remained on, then the power supply is most likely not delivering the necessary voltage or amperage. If the LED did not come on at all, then the LaserWriter logic board is very probably faulty.

If the green LED on the switch board behaved as it should, then shift your attention to the other three LEDs mounted on the front panel of the printer. The green should have begun flashing immediately that the printer received power and continued throughout the entire warm-up cycle.

The yellow LED should have begun to flash at longer intervals about 30 seconds into the warm-up and, after about 10 to 11 flashes, the test page should have been processed.

After the test page is ejected, the green should have become steady and the yellow extinguished. The red should not have lighted at all. If the red LED did light, then the paper path has some obstruction or the printer has a defect in the pathway sensors. If the yellow was steady rather then flashing, then either the paper cassette was empty or missing. If either the green or yellow did not light, then check the cable that connects the Video input/output on the logic board to the connector J-202 on the DC controller board. Are all of the wires of the cable making uninterrupted contact? Are the connectors locked into place by the plastic locking levers on the respective boards? Are the connectors properly positioned with respect to the keying on their sides? (Remember, the LaserJet cable must be flipped over at the LaserWriter end to make the correct connection.)

If reseating the cable connectors or rewiring the cable does not result in a test page, then the problem might be in either the LaserWriter PCB or in the DC controller. Disconnect the Video I/O cable from the LaserWriter board and turn on the printer. If the green LED on the front panel performs as expected, flashing for about $1^1/2$ to 2 minutes and then becoming steady, try printing a test grid by pressing the TEST PRINT button located at the rear of the left end panel. This should force the printing of a page of straight, parallel lines running the length of the paper. If this page is printed, then the problem is probably not with the DC controller, although the actual connector at J-201 still might remain under suspicion. Therefore, before having a service technician check out the LaserWriter board, run a continuity check on the pin connections of the DC controller board connector J-201. This can be done with a volt-ohm meter, set to ohms and then touching the test leads to each pin of the connector and to its solder point on the bottom of the circuit board. It is necessary to remove the board to make this check; removal is accomplished simply by taking out the screws and squeezing the nylon mounting locks until the board is free. Disconnect all of the plugs from the board and proceed to check connector J-201. If all is well there, then the problem is very likely in the LaserWriter logic board.

In practice, the only portion of the LaserWriter board that is amenable to user service is the ROM set. If you have a problem with the ROM, then replacing the chips with a known good set will usually solve any problem. However, as this can be an expensive way to run a check on the board, it is probably much more economical to simply have the board tested by inserting it into another printer. This does not guarantee that the board is 100%, but it can help to indicate whether the ROM chips and the basic circuitry of the board are operating. It is here that a discrepancy between Apple and other brand logic board power supplies can be revealed. Some

LaserWriter logic/interface board power supplies are rather more powerful than the board specifications require, and these power supplies can drive a board that will balk at a normal power source. The cause of this, as has been discussed earlier, is the burning of the resistors that act as filters for the I/O connections. Replacement of the resistor packs can bring the board back into compliance with the specifications.

Other faults in the LaserWriter board are not within the range of skills that you as a reader are expected to have to use this book. Only a service technician who is thoroughly familiar with the LaserWriter circuit architecture could be expected to be able to discover and repair the board. Be certain that you give the repair technician a full report of the board's behavior and of the the tests that you have been able to run yourself, because this can save the technician a considerable amount of time and you the money that redundant tests would have consumed. The more possible causes of failure that you can eliminate before seeking service and the more complete the information you can provide about the board and the printer in which it was installed, the easier it will be for the repair to be effected quickly and at a lower price.

Chapter 11

ROM upgrades

The LaserWriter logic boards have sixteen ROM sockets. Indeed, the only difference between a LaserWriter One and a LaserWriter Plus can be found in those sockets.

The earliest LaserWriters used two banks of eight 256K ROMs containing the Adobe PostScript interpreter and four Adobe typefaces. The LaserWriter Plus uses those same sockets to hold 512K chips, for one megabyte of revised PostScript and seven more typefaces. At the introduction of the Plus, Apple started using the higher density ROM chips for the LaserWriter One as well, thus leaving one bank of sockets unoccupied. Therefore, three configurations of the ROM chips can be found: All sockets filled with 256K chips, all filled with 512K chips, or half filled with 512K chips.

Apart from the chip configuration differences, the PostScript language has undergone maintenance and performance enhancements of PostScript since the first chips were burned. At any rate, a LaserWriter can become a LaserWriter Plus simply by replacing ROMs. The ROM replacement is the only component level alteration that the ordinary user himself will feel competent to perform on the logic board.

Apple sells LaserWriter upgrade kits for $799 through their authorized dealers. The price includes removal of the old chips and installation of the new ones. This is the surest way of receiving the latest and, presumably, best revision of the interpreter. It is surely the most expensive way. And the dealer will take your old chips. He will call it Apple's corporate trade-in policy, but it is stealing, all the same. The chips belong to you, regardless of the Adobe licensing agreement with Apple.

The better path to an upgrade is through an after-market reseller, such as Pre-Owned Electronics. They sell the PostScript Version 38 kits for about $200 – $400, and they do not creep into your home at night and purloin your old chips. The upgrade consists of merely prying out the current occupants of the sockets, storing them safely away in a static-free environment and inserting the replacement chips in their stead. The old chips can be kept for backup or resold.

To remove any chip from its socket is a tricky business. Using a forceps-like chip extraction tool is the safest method (Fig. 11-1), because it places the least amount of stress upon the various points of contact, that is, the chip's legs, the socket, and the solder points on the circuit board. If you do not have a tool, then the chip can be lifted from its socket by alternately prying up the ends, until it is loose and can be pulled free manually. The old chips should be placed in either a static-proof plastic tube, on a nonconductive foam mat, or wrapped in aluminum foil to protect them from static discharges. It is a good idea to use a grounding strap or mat before handling the new chips, and then they should leave your hand only to be inserted into their sockets or to be placed again into their shipping container.

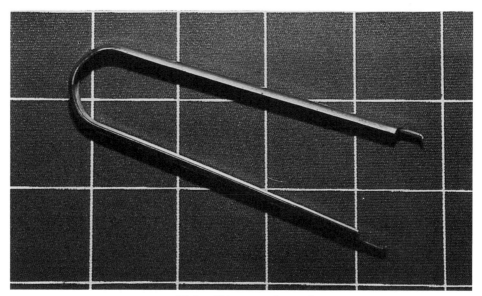

11-1 Chip extraction tool.

When new, a chip's pins or legs have a slightly splayed attitude, and they must usually be bent into the full 90° position before the chip can be socketed. Although there are specialized tools for this purpose, the straightening can be accomplished quite simply by holding the chip edgewise on a flat surface and exerting enough of a rocking pressure on the legs to bend them perpendicular to the chip's body (Fig. 11-2). When the legs on each side have been so treated, the chip will very likely slip into the socket without the application of undue force. Be certain that the end notch on the top side of the chip is oriented correctly with the corresponding notch on the socket, lest the chip be socketed backwards. There should be some resistance as the chip is inserted, but be careful that no pin is crumpled or bent during the insertion. When all the chips have been installed, a LaserWriter Plus has been created.

11-2 Rocking the chip gently in direction of arrows will straighten the bowed legs.

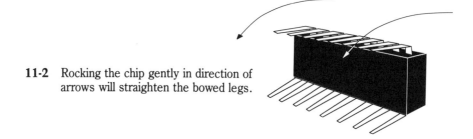

Chapter 12

Converting the Canon SX and later engines

The SX laser engine was designed by Canon specifically as the basis for a laser printer, unlike the CX which had sprouted out of the company's copier family. The new engine was smaller, lighter, and used less toner than the older CX. The SX engine made good some of the weaknesses of the CX, providing true, even blacks and heavier strokes in the smaller sizes of some type faces, which had been criticized for their frailness in the previous engine.

Not all that was done was an improvement, however. While small type became denser, it also became less elegant, and clotting of closed letters became evident. Of more concern to some was the sacrifice of the smooth transitions between gradations of gray in order to obtain the universally praised blacks. This meant that there were now visible bands in what had been previously well blended ranges between white and black. Worse still, for the many who had acquired the frugal habit of refilling their toner cartridges, the new, smaller toner cartridges were much less resistant to drum scratches, and the new toner formula, which was primarily responsible for the deep blacks, was perceptibly abrasive, further shortening the life expectancy of the cartridge drum.

All things considered, depending upon the individual's applications for the laser printer, the advantages outweighed the disadvantages for some and did not for others. However, because Canon had shifted all of its manufacturing capacity to the new machine, the question of whether one preferred the old to the new became moot. Apple and Hewlett-Packard shipped only new versions of their LaserWriters and LaserJets, and other OEMs either adopted the Canon engine in order to maintain backward and forward compatibility with the standard or struck off on their own by utilizing engines from Ricoh, Casio, or others, hoping to make a virtue of the difference.

The SX engine's dimensions make it less user intimidating than its predecessor. It is about 18 inches from left to right, 19 inches from front to back, 9 inches high, and weighs in at approximately 51 pounds, depending upon its plastic incarnation. It is, therefore, both lighter by 20 pounds and shorter by 4 inches than the CX.

It opens in a manner similar to the original, although the latch has been moved from the right front end to the top right corner. The paper path is designed so that face-up copy can be delivered to a flip-down tray in the rear of the printer, a straight-through pathway, or face down to a tray in the top of the printer's lid, a lazy U-shaped pathway. The mechanical and electronic functions of the printing process are identical in principle to those in the CX engine, although the individual components have been reconfigured for compactness.

SX engine choices

These engines are derivatives of the SX engine.

Canon LPB-2

The Canon version of its own engine is akin to the overlooked Canon LPB-CX laser printer, in that it is largely unnoticed in the laser printer marketplace. It is a LaserJet Plus compatible with Epson commands thrown in, and it presents itself as a lower cost, lower profile competitor for that series of printers.

HP LaserJet II

Typically, although virtually identical to the Canon machine, the HP LaserJet Series II far outdistances all other versions of the SX engine in sales (Fig. 12-1). It was cheaper than the Series I and provided more memory and greater typographic flexibility. Building upon the reputation and installed base of the Series I, the Series II extended HP's lead in the laser printer market, although the superiority of the Post-Script-based machines as true imagesetters had become clear. The HP printers were the standard draft animals of the computer based office publishing system, bearing the largest portion of the daily harvest of printed matter for both internal and broadcast distribution. PostScript printers were more and more being used for graphic and complex typographic presentations, as well as for small run bound matter formerly produced in printshops, but the HP LaserJet was the computer equivalent to the office Underwood of the pre-electronic office: It was ubiquitous and universally imitated.

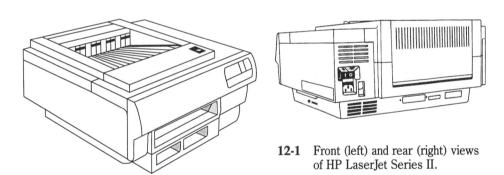

12-1   Front (left) and rear (right) views of HP LaserJet Series II.

Others

Naturally, imitation is easier if one starts with the same basic materials, and Canon had no objection to selling its SX engines to whomever desired to purchase them in large quantities for development of their own HP compatibles. The Japanese office equipment company, Brother, did exactly that, producing a printer, the HL8, which is practically indistinguishable from the Hewlett-Packard Series II and offers more features at a lower price.

Apple LaserWriters II

Apple Computer introduced its new LaserWriters II in 1987. The three models from which to choose were the SC, the NT, and the NTX.

SC

The SC was the surprising member of the family in that it was not a PostScript intelligent device. Even more surprising was the fact that it had only a SCSI (*small computer systems interface*) port through which to connect to the host computer, effectively limiting its use to owners of Macintoshes, and then only to those owning a Plus or later model. The SC could be upgraded to an NT or NTX by sliding in a new interface/logic board to replace the original. The external interface connectors were integral with the logic board itself, after the fashion of the Macintoshes, so that no internal cabling was needed. The board simply slipped into a slot in the bottom of the machine and the LaserWriter was transformed.

The SC was almost immediately derided for everything except its upgrade compatibility. The price was too high, the lack of PostScript was inexcusable, and the fact that it could not exist on a network meant that it offered nothing to the public that could not be obtained more cheaply from many other sources.

In particular, it was compared to the General Computer Corporation's Personal Laser Printer and found to be wanting. The SC did not use outline fonts, while the PLP used licensed outlines from Bitstream, which emulated very nicely the Adobe typefaces found in the ''real'' LaserWriters. The SC was stuck with using bit-mapped faces that required the user to install immense font files into the computer's operating system, so that the printer could then reduce the larger sizes for the print-out. No typographical effects were possible. Most of the programs that had become standard fare on the Macintosh would print to the SC, but the most important ones, that is those that used PostScript as their native tongue, would not print on the SC. Meanwhile, General Computer had made every effort to create drivers for those programs that had PostScript-specific printing requirements. And the PLP was several hundred dollars cheaper than the SC, and it, too, could be upgraded to Post-Script. The consensus was that SC was not a good deal.

NT

The LaserWriter II NT is very little different from the machine it replaced, the LaserWriter Plus. It offers two megabytes of RAM and the latest version of Post-Script in ROM. The NT is based on the Canon SX engine, as are all three LaserWriters II, but it is no speedier nor any more capable than the Plus. The extra $1/2$ megabyte of memory comes in handy for downloaded typefaces, but the amount of RAM is fixed and cannot be expanded. The new PostScript is optimized for greater speed, but the same PostScript can be added to the Plus. It is a middle-of-the-road machine, rather overpriced when compared to PostScript conversant printers from other sources.

NTX

The top-of-the-line machine from Apple, the NTX, is worthy of the LaserWriter heritage. It exemplifies the virtues and vices that the original LaserWriters established as hallmarks of Apple, that is, high performance and high price.

While containing exactly the same engine as its two siblings, and using exactly the same version of PostScript as the NT, the NTX is really in another class. It is expandable beyond the needs (and means) of almost any private user. It is among the fastest of laser printers, coming close to fulfilling the 8 pages per minute rating of the Canon engine. And it carries a hefty price of $6600.

Building an NTX equivalent is really beyond the scope of this book. Because the architecture of the NTX is so radically advanced from that of the original LaserWriter, it would not be possible to kludge together a work-alike machine from common parts. No doubt it would be possible to add an accelerator to the 68000 CPU, upgrading it to a 68020 or a 68030, but this would require specialized hardware and a rewritten ROM to handle the instruction differences and timing—not to mention a replacement of a crystal here and there. The SCSI could probably be added through some sort of Killy clip-on apparatus, but again the ROM would have to be replaced to make it possible to use the devices that might be attached through the SCSI. Memory expansion to match that of the NTX would also use similar unwieldy solutions involving snap-on and ROM replacement parts, and are equally impracticable. However, a description of its architecture and capabilities follows, if only to tantalize.

The NTX logic board differs from previous Apple LaserWriter boards in that it bears more of a kinship with the Macintosh II series of computers than with the earlier Macs. The NTX has SIMM (*single inline memory modules*) slots instead of soldered banks of RAM chips. This means that the NTX can address up to 12 megabytes of RAM if all of the slots are filled with high-density RAM modules. Such a prodigious amount of RAM is really useful only for extensive RAM caching of typefaces, but a corporation or quick-printing house could find that space invaluable for the instant access that it gives to downloaded headline fonts and special character sets. And, as any PostScript graphic can be defined as a font character, it is possible that the extra RAM could be filled with fonts consisting entirely of complex PostScript graphics.

In addition, the NTX has a SCSI port. Unlike the SCSI of the SC, this port is meant, not for connection to the host, but for the attachment of a dedicated hard drive. The hard drive can contain thousands of PostScript typefaces, all of them available at any time to the printer without the necessity of using valuable space on the user's drive or requiring that they be downloaded from the host. If a large enough drive is installed, then the printer can cache enormous numbers of typefaces for instantaneous use, rather than having to reconstruct a previously used and discarded font. Perhaps of equal significance to this practically unlimited typographic potential is the fact that the CPU of the NTX is the Motorola 68020, operating with a 68881 math coprocessor. This allows the basic number crunching of PostScript to proceed at speeds that push the 8 ppm limit of the engine, nearly doubling the throughput of the NT or Plus. Complex graphic images that might take minutes for an ordinary printer to render are completed in mere seconds by the NTX. It is an extraordinary machine.

QMS JetScript

Alternatives to the standard Apple had established were more than ever needed, because the retail prices of LaserWriters remained extremely high, from about $3200 for the uninspiring NT to about $4600 for the much desired NTX.

Fortunately, PostScript clones and PostScript compatibles were produced by Ricoh, Qume, Brother, and others, and sold well at prices between $2500 to $3500, which was still relatively high when compared to the LaserJets. Real Postscript printers from companies such as QMS were usually aimed at the high end of the market and gave little price relief to the single user.

Fortunately, following up on their PS-Jet+ conversion kits, the QMS subsidiary, Laser Connection, introduced a kit that would upgrade a LaserJet to PostScript (Fig. 12-2). Unfortunately, the price of adding this upgrade (about $1600) brought the total printer cost level with Apple's street price for a LaserWriter NT. Worse, the conversion consists of a system, rather than a single controller board replacement, which requires that an IBM PC or PC clone be part of the printer set-up. A board is installed in the printer and an interface card is added in one of the computer's slots to give the host access to the printer. This totally prohibits the Macintosh, the most numerous PostScript printer driving host, from use of the system. PostScript printers ought by definition be free-standing devices. The advantage in the systemic approach, at least for QMS, lies in the fact that fully three-fourths of all computers in use are IBM PCs or are PC compatible.

Apart from this gaffe, the PostScript upgrade is attractive, if you have a PC available. It carries 3Mb of RAM and a very-high-speed (57,600 baud) dedicated serial port through which communications can take place, making the PC a very productive platform for PostScript page makeup. If the upgrade can be purchased at a lower price, as is sometimes offered, then it is a very viable alternative, and the only true PostScript upgrade worth using.

Cartridges and other solutions

In 1989 Pacific Data Products began to offer a PostScript emulator for the Hewlett-Packard LaserJet Series II printers. The emulator, PhoenixPage from Phoenix Technologies, is contained in a standard size HP font cartridge and plugs into the slot in

12-2 QMS Laser Connection JetScript PostScript conversion system for Canon SX type laser engines.

the printer's lid. The real market price is about $450 – $475. It is claimed that it supports downloaded Type 1 Adobe type faces. Because Adobe has placed a one machine per package lock on their Type 1 faces and no other current emulator can use the encrypted hints of those faces, this is a significant claim. AppleTalk is supported as an extra cost option.

This is a qualified solution, however, because it applies only to Series II and later series printers and only to the HP brand. When the price of the cartridge is added to the price of the printer, the solution becomes less attractive, and emulations, however refined, cannot be simultaneously 100% compatible and legal. A real PostScript printer based on the CX engine can be assembled for less. There is the additional problem, perhaps more severe, of possible incompatibility between the Phoenix Page cartridge and other third-party and HP optional hardware for the Series II. The Phoenix Page cartridge overrides the native HP interface controller and disables all other logical devices plugged into the second Series II cartridge slot, meaning, for instance, that the printer cannot be on a PC network at the same time that it is functioning as a PostScript compatible. Other as yet undetermined effects of this supervisory usurpation might exist.

In the meanwhile, more software vendors had entered the PostScript clone market with their own versions of emulators. UltraScript was another QMS product, designed to run from Atari ST, Amiga, and IBM PC platforms. In the Macintosh world, Freedom of the Press appeared in 1989, giving PostScript imitation to any dot matrix printer. Not to be outshone, Adobe itself created Adobe Type Manager, a mild form of its own Display PostScript, a product that was a joint venture of Adobe and NeXT, the company founded by Steve Jobs, after his expulsion from Apple. Apple Computer, hoping to extend the WYSIWYG environment of the Macintosh by making the screen display more closely resemble the printed page, but reluctant to license yet another form of PostScript, especially a product that had been designed to run originally on the Jobs' computer, severed its ties to Adobe and sold its sizable stock holdings. Apple then teamed up with Microsoft, which, incidentally, it was concurrently suing for copyright infringement, to adapt a third-party PostScript clone to Apple's printers-in-planning, giving birth to TrueImage and TrueType.

The problem with all the software solutions remained, however, in the slowness and memory demands which they placed upon the computers themselves. Even Adobe Type Manager, which would run transparently on a one megabyte Macintosh Plus, was slow and memory hungry, forcing the owners of machines with less than 2 megabytes of RAM to either expand memory or buy a new machine with a faster throughput.

While you have plenty of alternatives to buying a PostScript printer based upon the SX engine and later engines such as the Canon LPB4 and HP LaserJet IIP, to actually convert an extant latter generation machine to PostScript remains a challenge. To date, the only affordable conversion method is by way of the somewhat limiting JetScript system for IBM and HP Vectra computers. The more convenient PostScript clone cartridge from Pacific Page supports both the Macintosh and IBM worlds, but, like all clones, it cannot be 100% compatible with the original and remain legal. Of course, you can at any time buy a logic board from Apple, at a cost of $2400, and install it in an SX, but this hardly seems to be a reasonable choice, since the final cost of the printer would equal that of a new LaserWriter NT and exceed that of competing printers by about $1000. What is needed is a way to interface a CX logic board to the SX engine.

A theoretical solution

If you consult the accompanying table (Table 12-1) and compare it to that in chapter 4 (Table 4-5), it appears that it is possible to add a first generation PostScript logic board to the second generation engine. In other words, the same Apple LaserWriter board that was installed in a stock CX laser engine in chapter 4 might be interfaced to a LaserJet II or other SX type of printer. The signals required and generated by each of the engines are sufficiently similar that you might attempt to construct an externally mounted enclosure for the logic board and to connect it through a custom wiring harness to the power supply and DC controller of the SX printer. The CX logic board produces both positive and negative signals for most of the printer functions, while

Table 12-1. SX DC controller J-205 connector pin assignments.

Pin	Signal	Signal	Pin
A1	Signal ground	Printer power ready ($-$)	A2
A3	Vertical sync request ($-$)	Status ($-$)	A4
A5	Command busy ($-$)	Vertical sync ($-$)	A6
A7	Video signal ($-$)	C Clock ($-$)	A8
A9	-5 volt	NC	A10
B1	Beam deatect ($-$)	Ready ($-$)	B2
B3	Status busy ($-$)	P Clock	B4
B5	Print ($-$)	Controller power ready ($-$)	B6
B7	Command ($-$)	NC	B8
B9	$+24$ volt	Field ground	B10

the SX logic boards use only the negative signals. Therefore, by connecting the respective negative sources of the DC controller and LaserWriter logic board, it should be possible to drive the newer engine.

The signals of the LaserWriter logic board would be drawn from the Video I/O connector, where the pin assignments would be the reverse of the LaserJet cabling (remember the twist applied to the cable for orientation to the CX's DC controller) or a straight through trace if you are starting from scratch. In either case, the 24 volt and 5 volt lines can be ignored.

That is the theoretical link, but even if it does work, which has not been proved, is there any real reason to attempt it? The print quality of the CX engine is generally equal to that of the SX engine and is, in some respects, superior. The print speed is the same. The SX engine is smaller and lighter, but the CX engine is cheaper and much more easily adapted to PostScript than is the second generation machine. Unless you already own a well-worn SX engine and are willing to risk a LaserWriter board in the trial, it does not make much sense to look for ways to begin building a PostScript printer from a basic SX engine. Of course, if you can manage to find a bargain price for the QMS JetScript (it sometimes is available for as little as $795), and you already have a LaserJet Series II and an IBM PC or clone, then it is well worth the money to make the upgrade. Similarly, if a sudden plethora of LaserWriter II boards appear in the used parts' market, then it makes perfect sense to mount one in an SX machine. But the first happenstance is rare, and the likelihood of the second is not within the capacity of any microcomputer to calculate. Stay with the CX engine.

The third-generation machines are intriguing, for their size and price are both historically small. However, neither HP's RAM expansion nor its PostScript cartridge option are inexpensive, and the third-party substitutes still do not bring true PostScript within the same price range of the converted CX. Even the Texas Instruments Micro Laser, which delivers PostScript for about $2000, is $400 more. Stay with the CX.

Chapter 13

Parts lists, sources, and general buying tips

The most important parts for the conversion are, of course, the LaserWriter logic board and the Canon CX laser engine. These fluctuate in both their available quantities and their prices, but the careful and persistent buyer should be able to find each component at or below the prices suggested here.

LaserWriter boards and Canon engines

You should not have to pay more than about $500 for a reconditioned LaserJet Series I or other Canon CX, and $1100 for the LaserWriter board itself. In all, additional parts and supplies should be obtainable for less than $100, putting the final cost of a true 8 pages per minute PostScript printer with serial and AppleTalk interfaces below $1700, a savings of $700 – $800 over the price of an off-the-shelf PostScript printer. If you go to the extra expense of purchasing the Hewlett-Packard service manual for the LaserJet 2686A/D, $29.95, you will have all that is necessary to completely and competently maintain the printer almost indefinitely.

I strongly advise that all the necessary parts be procured at about the same time, so that any failures can be detected and isolated while vendor guarantees are still in effect.

LaserWriter logic boards and ROM sets

The LaserWriter logic/interface board is the part for which there is no substitute, and it must be secured before all else. If at all possible, have the board tested thoroughly by a knowledgeable technician and obtain a written warranty before putting down your money.

Genuine Apple boards possess the Apple logo and the Apple Computer name to the right of the M68000 CPU and the Apple Computer copyright and part number silk-screened on the upper right-hand corner of the board. Three configurations of ROM are to be seen: All sockets filled with low-density chips (earliest LaserWriters One), all sockets filled with high-density chips (LaserWriters Plus), and half of the sockets filled with high-density chips (late model LaserWriters One).

Vendors

Becker Computer Systems
405 Murray Hill Parkway
East Rutherford, NJ 07073
(201) 670-0505

Maya Computer
Box 680
Waitsfield, VT 05673
(800) 541-2318

Pre-Owned Electronics
30 Clematis Avenue
Waltham, MA 02154
(800) 274-5343
(617) 891-6851
(617) 891-3556 (fax)

Simmons Microsystems
6714 Market Street
Upper Darby, PA 19082
(215) 352-6883
(215) 352-6975 (fax)

Shreve Systems
2421 Malcolm Street
Shreveport, LA 71108
(800) 227-3971
(318) 635-1121
(318) 865-2006 (fax)
(318) 636-4887 (BBS)

Other sources

You need not rely solely on the resources of third-party vendors and resellers listed in the previous section. Local computer shows and fairs occasionally yield boards and other parts. The local Apple dealer can sometimes be persuaded to sell a board that he has no need of as a repair substitute, although this is seldom the case. And the local user's groups or bulletin boards are likely to know of any private parties with boards to sell. Even a flea market can sometimes have surprising wares for sale.

Canon CX engines

The sources for the Canon CX laser engine are more numerous than those for the LaserWriter boards, because the controls that Apple places on it products are happily absent from Canon's marketing plan.

Vendors

Computer Products and Peripheral Unlimited
18 Granite Street
Haverhill, MA 01830
(617) 372-8637

Equipment Resources, Inc.
1833 14th Street N.W.
Washington, D.C. 20009
(202) 338-2429
(202) 338-2462 (fax)

Exsel, Inc.
2200 Brighton-Henrietta Townline Road
Rochester, NY 14623
(800) 624-2001
(716) 212-8770
(716) 212-8624 (fax)

Hargadorn Computer
3517-C Edison Way
Menlo Park, CA 94025
(800) 736-3062
(415) 364-8954
(415) 364-8956 (fax)
Note that Hargadorn also might be a source for low-price QMS JetScript conversion kits.

Hi-Tech Computer Products
6500 NW 15th Avenue
Fort Lauderdale, FL 33309
(800) 940-6991
(305) 977-6991
(305) 977-0209 (fax)

Printer Works
3481 Arden Road
Hayward, CA 94545
(800) 225-6116
(415) 887-6116
(415) 786-0589 (fax)

Ted Dasher & Associates
4117 2nd Avenue
South Birmingham, AL 35222
(205) 591-4747
(205) 591-1108 (fax)

Vision Investment Recovery
11 Sixth Road
Woburn, MA 01801
(800) 242-5224
(800) 287-3372
(617) 935-1886 (fax)

Other sources

The same suggestions I made for finding LaserWriter boards apply to the Canon CX, with the addition of the local newspaper. The "Miscellaneous For Sale," "Computers For Sale," and "Business Equipment For Sale" classified columns should all be examined for possible bargains. The Yellow Pages of the telephone directories of larger cities also should not be overlooked. The classifieds of *Computer Shopper* are a prime source of vendors for both the CX engine in its various forms and the LaserWriter logic board.

Power supplies

The purchase of a power supply is necessary only if you are converting the NEC engine. All other forms of the CX engine have been provided with the logic board power supply. The very easiest method of adding a power supply that is certain to be compatible is to purchase the Hewlett-Packard interface board power supply components:

- The interface power supply Printed Circuit board, part number RH3-2004-000CN.
- The interface power supply transformer, part number RH3-0014-000CN.
- The line filter, part number RF1-0190-000CN.

Hewlett-Packard Company, Inc.
Direct Marketing Division
1326 Kifer Road
P.O. Box 60008
Sunnyvale, CA 94088
(800) 538-8787

The second option is to buy the Apple LaserWriter power supply from either Pre-Owned Electronics or another dealer in Apple parts. Their addresses are listed in the section devoted to LaserWriter logic boards.

Lastly, you can chose the path of least expense and purchase or build an external power supply. The choices here are not so clear, due to the very stringent requirements of the logic board. The Jameco switching power supply, FCS604A, priced at $39.95 – $44.95, works, but it is likely to cause some interference due to the noise that it generates. Check out power supplies from the following vendors:

B.G. Micro
P.O. Box 280298
Dallas, TX 75228
(214) 271-5546
(214) 271-2462 (fax)

Jameco Electronics
1355 Shoreway Road
Belmont, CA 94002
(415) 592-8097

JDR Microdevices
2233 Branham Lane
San Jose, CA 95124
(800) 538-5000

Lolir Computer
2741 Beltline Road #111
Carrolton, TX 75006
(214) 416-5155

Mendelson Electronics
340 East First Street
Dayton, OH 45402
(800) 422-3525
(513) 461-3525
(513) 461-3391 (fax)

Timeline, Inc.
1490 West Artesia Boulevard
Gardena, CA 90247
(800) 872-8878
(800) 223-9977
(213) 217-8912
(213) 532-6304 (fax)

Cables and connectors

Cables and connectors can be bought at any Radio Shack electronics store (look in the telephone book for the one near you). If, for some reason, Radio Shack does not have the parts and cannot get them, the following vendors will oblige:

Altex Electronics
300 Breesport
San Antonio, TX 78216
(800)-531-5369
(512)-349-8795

Dalco Electronics
223 Pioneer Boulevard
Springboro, OH 45066
(800)-445-5342
(513)-743-8042
(513)-743-9251 (fax)

Digi-Key Corporation
P.O. Box 677
Thief River Falls, MN 56701
(800)-344-4539

Jameco Electronics
1355 Shoreway Road
Belmont, CA 94002
(415)-592-8097

Ora Electronics
9410 Owensmouth Avenue
Chatsworth, CA 91313
(800)-423-5336
(818)-718-8626 (fax)

Redmond Cable
17371-A1 N.E. 67 Court
Redmond, WA 98052
(206)-882-2009

Manuals

The indispensable service manual for the Canon CX laser engine is the Hewlett-Packard 2686A/D Printer Service Manual, PN# 02686-90920 for $29.95.

Hewlett-Packard Company, Inc.
Direct Marketing Division
1326 Kifer Road
P.O. Box 60008
Sunnyvale, CA 94088
(800)-538-8787

The Apple Laserwriter kit of manuals and disks called "Inside LaserWriter" goes for $75. The manual alone, *Apple LaserWriter Reference Manual* goes for $19.50. Both are available through a local Apple dealer or from Apple Computer.

Apple Computer, Inc.
20525 Mariani Avenue
Cupertino, CA 95014
(408)-996-1010

Adobe has published several PostScript manuals and tutorials, including: *PostScript Language Program Design*, *PostScript Reference Manual*, and *PostScript Tutorial and Cookbook*.

Adobe Systems, Inc.
1585 Charleston Road
P.O. Box 7900
Mountain View, CA 94039-7900
(415)-961-0911

Toner refills and refilling materials

Toner cartridge refillers can be found advertised in the telephone book or in the newspapers of every medium-sized town or city in the country. Failing that, any of the general interest computer magazines on the store racks have half a dozen refillers among the advertisers. Toner refilling materials are, however, less common.

Table 13-1. Parts for interfaces, switches, and LED indicators.

Part	Amount	RS part number	Price each
Ribbon cable 36 conductor	6 feet	278-774	4.69
IDC header 34 pin	3	276-1525	2.49
Dual mini board	1	276-148	1.39
9 pin female DB-mini connector	1	276-1428	1.19
Heat shrink tubing	1	278-1627	1.79
Red LED T 1³/₄ size	1	276-041	.69 (pack of 2)
Yellow LED T 1³/₄ size	1	276-021	.79 (pack of 2)
Green LED T 1³/₄ size	2	276-022	.79 (pack of 2)
LED holders T 1³/₄ size	4	276-079	.59 (pack of 5)
150 ohm 1/4 watt resistors	3	271-1312	.39 (pack of 5)
Female quick-disconnects	2	64-3039	1.29 (pack of 8)
Zip cord 18 gauge	3 ft.	278-864	2.99 (30 ft. spool)
Dip switch 4 position	1	275-1304	1.39

Chenesko Products
62 N. Coleman Road
Centereach, NY 11720
(516) 736-7977
(516) 732-4650 (fax)

Lazer Products
12741 East Kaley Avenue, S130
Englewood, CO 80111
(303) 792-5277

Thompson & Thompson
23072 Lake Center Drive, Suite #100
El Toro, CA 92630
(714) 855-3838

Appendix A

How it works

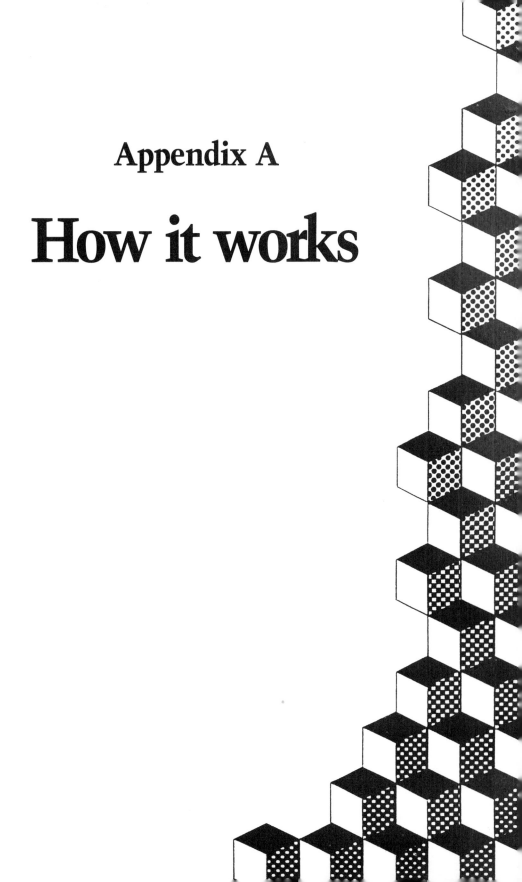

This section describes how various processes in your PostScript laser printer work. These descriptions are designed to help you determine what you are getting and what you want from your printer.

PostScript

Each point size must be individually rendered as a raster image by the interpreter in the best resolution of the printer, but every size is calculated from the same set of vectors. A 12 point Courier A printed on a LaserJet using the LaserJet's bit-mapped face will be identical to its PostScript printed counterpart on the LaserWriter, because the LaserJet has a 12 point Courier predetermined bit-mapped typeface specially designed for 300 dpi. The PostScript machine must first calculate the outline of the character at 12 points, then fill it in with dots. So at this one size and one typeface, the LaserJet has an advantage in speed.

The real test comes when a required for font size does not have a corresponding predefined bit map already in place in the printer. The LaserJet must then expand the bit map for the next closest point size to fill the request, resulting in "jaggies" or "aliasing," the staircase effect of mismatched bit maps and point sizes, while the LaserWriter will take the same outline from which it developed the 12 point size and run the same calculations for the new size, filling in the dots only after the smoothest possible form has been constructed.

PostScript effects

Text effects in PostScript are achieved with relative ease through manipulation of the font matrix or through the application of graphic's effects to the font outline.

PostScript typefaces are defined by a six parameter matrix attached to the command [ ] makefont. For example, in Times-Roman findfont [20 0 0 20 0 0] makefont setfont, the first parameter establishes the font characters' width in points, the second the inclination or declination of the characters from the horizontal, the third their slant or angle from the perpendicular, the fourth the characters' height in points, the fifth their horizontal offset, and the sixth their vertical offset (for subscripts and superscripts). Negative values can be specified for the parameters with the result being the reverse or inverse of the corresponding positive values. Thus, type can be made to print as a right-to-left mirror image by making the first parameter negative, e.g., Times-Roman findfont [-20 0 0 20 0 0].

Graphic effects can also be applied to text. Use of the command ( ) setgray, for example, will allow printing of text in any available gray shade gradation between black (0) and white (1). Other graphic's effects applicable to text include binding to a path, usually a circle or arc (although any arbitrary line can be used), rotation around an axis, or spiralling, among others. Printed effects and some PostScript programming examples follow.

Inclined and shadowed text :

```
    /Times-Bold findfont [40 40 .577 mul 0 50 0 0] makefont setfont .75 setgray 100
300 moveto 1 0 (Incline and Shadow) ashow
    /Times-Bold findfont [40 40 -.577 mul 0 50 0 0] makefont setfont 0 setgray 100
300 moveto 1 0 (Incline and Shadow) ashow
    showpage
```

Reversed text :

```
    /Times-Bold findfont [ − 50 0 0 40 0 0] makefont setfont 400 400 moveto 1 0
(Print Reverse.) ashow
    showpage
```

Rotated text :

```
    initclip
    /Helvetica-Bold findfont [30 0 0 30 0 0] makefont setfont
    /ShowOutline {true charpath stroke} def
    /RotateCircle {30 30 330
    {gsave rotate 0 0 moveto (Rotate) ShowOutline grestore} for} def
    300 400 translate
    .5 setlinewidth
    RotateCircle 0 0 moveto (Rotate) true charpath
    gsave 0 setgray fill grestore
    stroke
    showpage
```

Slanted text:

```
/Times-Bold findfont [24 0 45 sin 45 cos div 24 mul 24 0 0] makefont setfont
(Slanted text.) show
showpage
```

Slanted text.

Other examples of what you can do with PostScript are shown below.

TrueType

Apple has used both bit-mapped and PostScript outline typefaces, but is making a break from Adobe in two ways. One, Apple is developing its own outline standard, the TrueType typefaces, which are constructed on the fly from formulae defined by quadratic equations. Theoretically, these typefaces will offer the same resolution independence as PostScript typefaces because both are mathematically, not graphically, defined. However, Adobe uses cubic splines as the basis for typeface definition, which use fewer control loci to delineate a curve than do quadratics. So the two standards will very likely not be compatible. Second, Apple and Microsoft, as often at odds as in accord, are sharing font technologies to create a PostScript clone called TrueImage for use in Apple's future laser printers. The problem with this, as with every other, clone is the proprietary nature of Adobe's Type 1 faces. Despite that Adobe has promised to release into the public domain the specifications for Type 1 faces, this does not mean that clone makers will be able to make their emulations compatible with those specifications.

Setting the EEPROM

Don Lancaster gives the form that PostScript meddling with the EEPROM should take. (See chapter 8 for cautions about setting the EEPROM.) It is also possible using this format to set the baud rate of the printer's serial port at any desired speed up to the 57,600 baud limit. This is useful primarily for Apple II users, although IBM users might choose to increase the baud rate to 19,200, which is the ceiling for serial communications on the PC. To further discourage this tampering with the EEPROM, I am obliged to note that the LaserWriters contain a password that must never be altered. It begins as 0 and should remain so. It was discovered by some to their regret that a change of this value disabled the board from printing permanently if they did not know how to reset the EEPROM. Some software, for copy protection and other nefarious reasons, also would access this password, and sometimes change it, seemingly at random. MacDraw in its earlier versions was known to be an an offender in this regard. Therefore, it is extremely risky for the ordinary user to venture into this territory without adequate preparation. (See ''Ask The Guru'' in the August 1987 *Computer Shopper* on page 322 and the November 1988 issue on pages 411-412.) The actual PostScript code for switching the printer to hardware handshaking using the RTS and DTR lines is as follows:

```
/dtron [severdict begin 0 exitserver statusdict begin 25 57600 4 setsccbatch 25
57600 4 setsccinteractive end] def
```

This code also sets the baud rate to 57600. Other values such as 19200 or 9600 can be substituted.

The code for switching back to the XON/XOFF protocol is:

```
/xonxoff [severdict begin 0 exitserver statusdict begin 25 57600 0 setsccbatch
25 57600 0 setsccinteractive end] def
```

Write white vs. write black

The fundamental difference between the write white and write black page printers is illustrated by Fig. A-1.

A-1   The difference in printing between write black (left) and write white (right) laser engines.

As can be seen, the write white engine fills unilluminated areas of the page with solid black. Because most pages are composed of white space, the spill over of black into white tends to cause a general muddiness and, in small point alphanumeric characters, a clotting that renders the text unattractive.

On the other hand, write black engines leave unilluminated areas white. Write black engines have less dense black fills due to the cropping of the edges of the pixels, while text appears much more crisp and can be reduced to smaller point sizes because of this same cropping. The minute lattice work of open spaces between black dots limits blacks to a shade of gray, although true grays are more evenly graduated than those from a write white machine.

To some extent the weakness of the CX blacks can be obviated by refilling toner cartridges with specially formulated toners and by increasing the developer voltage bias by adjustment of the print density setting to a lower number.

LED and liquid crystal engines

LED array printers are based upon an optical system that uses a bank or line of light emitting diodes, packed 300 or more to the inch, which are switched on or off to create a full raster scan line. Such an array requires less power and is cheaper to produce than a laser scanning unit, because there are no moving parts and LEDs have an inherently lower power draw than do laser diodes. However, the laser can be focused to a much smaller point than can the LED, with a greater resolution from the laser printer being the result.

Liquid crystal shutter (LCS) engines are similar in design to the LED printers, in that they have no moving parts in their optical system and are cheaper to build than laser engines. Like LED array engines, they also create an entire scan line at once. A line of liquid crystal shutter spans the width of the page, and each shutter is either opaque or transparent, blocking or passing light from a fluorescent source to the photoconductive drum. Again, as with the LED engines, potential resolution is less than that of a laser engine, and the speed with which the individual shutters can be switched from opaque to transparent and reversed tends to give laser printers an edge in the number of pages per minute that can be printed. Casio and Epson were early entrants in the LCS field of non-laser page printers.

Laser diode

The laser is really a *laser diode* (Fig. A-2), a miniaturized silicon version of the familiar gaseous lasers of science and science fiction, wherein it can do everything from piercing armor plate to transmitting minute digital data to the moon and back. The semiconductor laser is a diode consisting of a negative and a positive pole. When positive and negative charges meet, light is the product. Photons, or packets of light, bounce back and forth between the reflective surfaces, until an energy threshold is passed, when laser light is emitted.

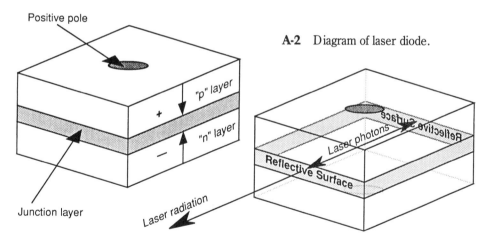

A-2 Diagram of laser diode.

Semiconductor lasers (Fig. A-3) called *heterojunction p-n devices* are comprised of electrically active layers grown upon a gallium arsenide (GaAs) substrate by a process called *epitaxy*. The negative (n) polar layer is a high-energy conduction band that produces a stream of electrons (electrons bear a negative charge). The positive (p) valence layer is a low-energy band in which "holes" are produced (a *hole* is

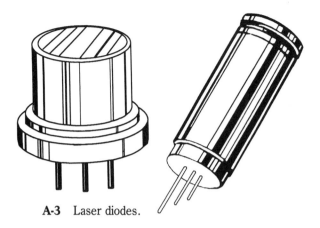

A-3 Laser diodes.

defined as the absence of an electron and carries a positive charge). When an electron collides with a hole, a photon of light energy is released. All photons produced in the laser diode are of the same wavelength and energy, as determined by the relative energy difference between the electron band and hole band. The photons are constrained electrically and optically within the collision layer until enough photons have accumulated to exceed a prescribed energy threshold, at which time laser light is emitted.

Laser diodes produce extremely low frequency infrared light, with wavelengths of 0.78 microns or less commonly in use. Light from the laser is made parallel by a collimation lens, which is part of the laser unit. The light then is reflected from the rotating hexagonal mirror, and each face creates one scan line. The reflected beam is focused by another lens, and a portion diverted into the beam detect fiber-optic cable, which carries it to beam detect module of the DC controller. This is a reference beam for the beginning of each scan line. The beam then passes to the curvature compensation lens, which provides correction for the difference in distance between the center and the ends of the drum as the beam is scanned from left to right. The beam next encounters the beam-to-drum prismatic mirror, which bends and reflects the light down onto the drum's surface as it traverses the length of the mirror; 33,600 lines are scanned per minute, 560 lines per second, covering an entire 8- × -10 inch page in approximately 5.36 seconds.

Laser diodes function best in a controlled temperature environment, so a thermostatically regulated heater is part of the scanning unit. Even though the beam is invisible and at a very low power, the focused beam can cause permanent eye damage.

Appendix B

Schemata

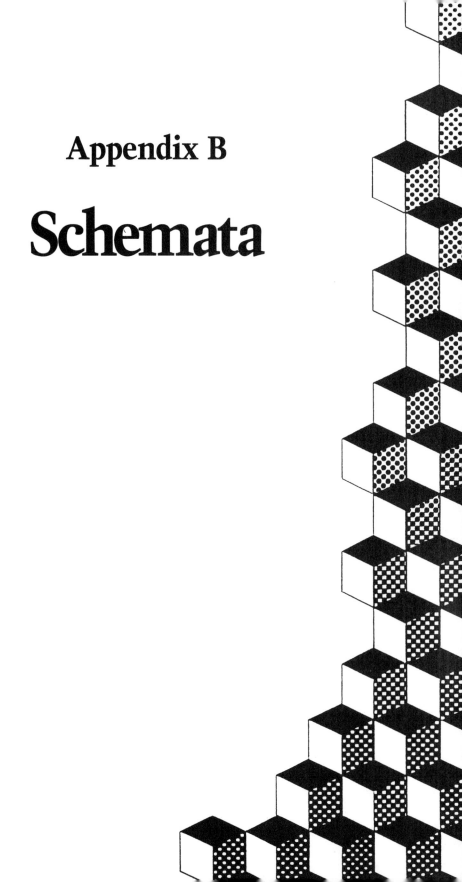

The schematics and diagrams included here are amplifications of subjects covered in the relevant chapters.

LaserWriter to computer cabling diagrams

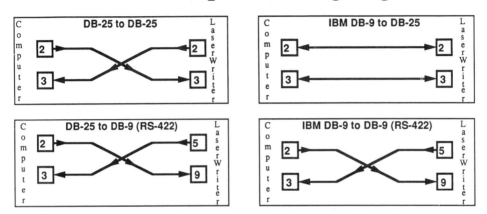

B-1 Simple serial cables for the IBM type computer to LaserWriter connection (Table 6-3).

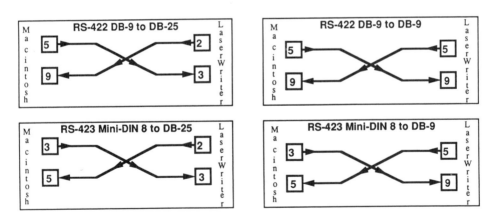

B-2 Simple serial cables for Macintosh to LaserWriter connection (Table 6-6).

RS-232/422 Handshaking
No Handshaking

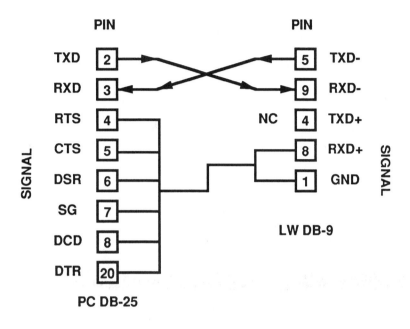

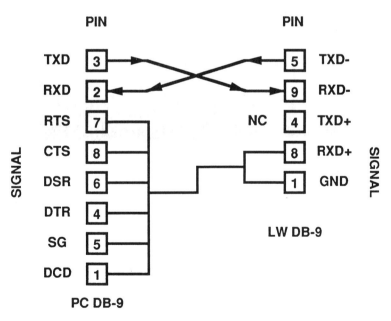

B-3 RS-232/422 handshaking and no handshaking diagrams (chapter 6).

RS-232 Handshaking
Null Modem

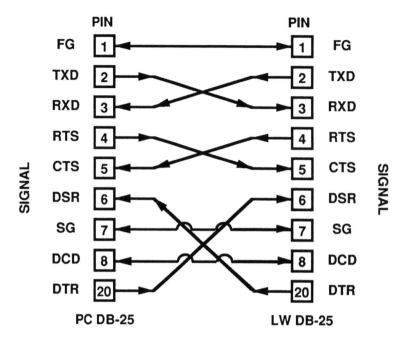

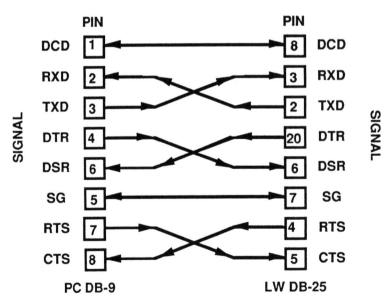

B-4 IBM DB-25 and DB-9 RS-232 handshaking and null modem diagrams (Tables 6-7 and 6-8, respectively).

RS-232 Handshaking

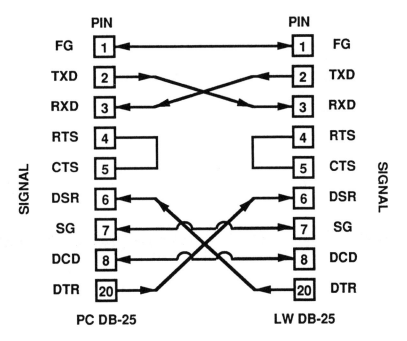

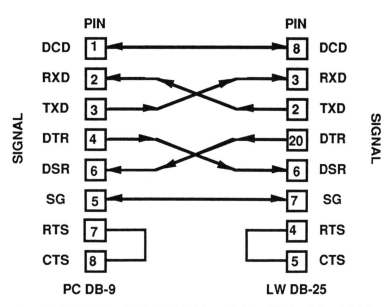

B-5 IBM DB-25 and DB-9 RS-232 handshaking (Tables 6-9 and 6-10).

RS-232 Handshaking

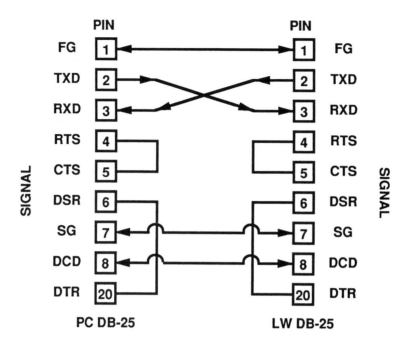

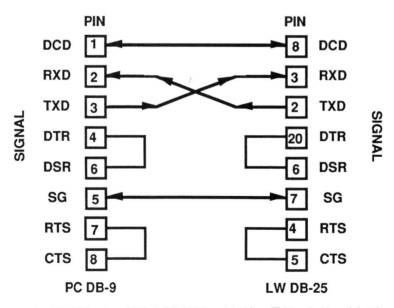

B-6   IBM DB-25 and DB-9 RS-232 handshaking (Tables 6-11 and 6-12).

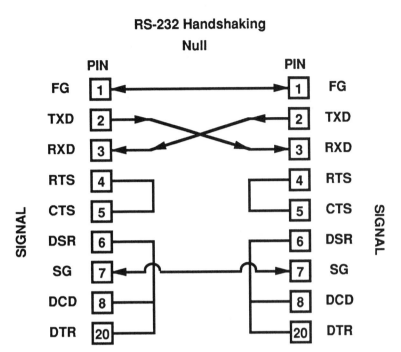

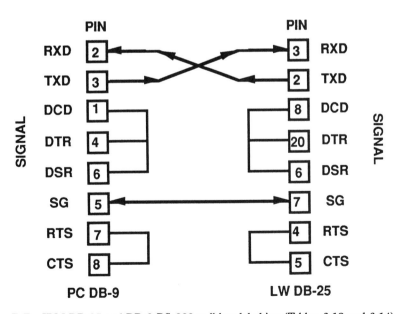

B-7 IBM DB-25 and DB-9 RS-232 null handshaking (Tables 6-13 and 6-14).

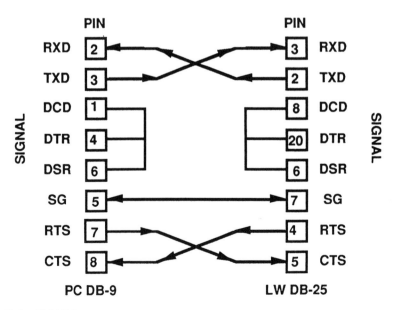

B-8 IBM DB-25 and DB-9 RS-232 full handshaking (Tables 6-15 and 6-16).

RS-232 Handshaking
No Handshaking

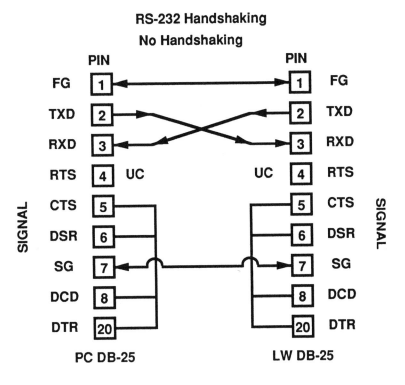

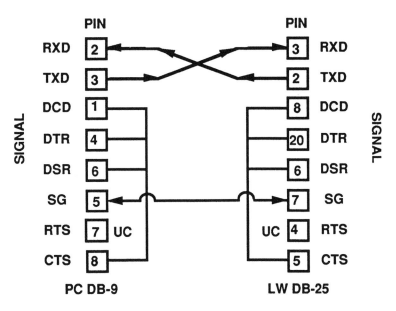

B-9 IBM DB-25 and DB-9 RS-232 no handshaking (Tables 6-17 and 6-18).

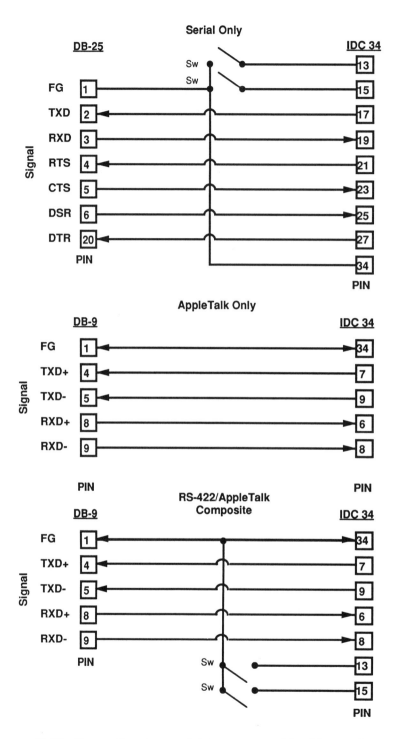

B-10 Types of interfaces and their connector wiring (chapter 4).

Composite interface switch and startup LED

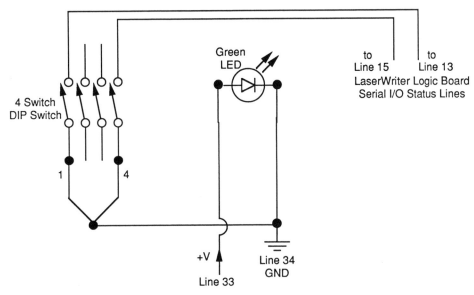

B-11 Mode switch schematic.

Status LEDs schematic

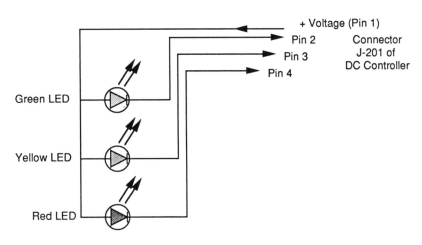

Status LED Schematic

B-12 LED status schematic.

Appendix C

General maintenance and troubleshooting

The cx engine is a complex piece of electronic and mechanical confectionery. Surprisingly, it is also remarkably reliable and resilient. It is one of those products that lives up to its design specifications and to your own expectations. However, every system, however well thought out and well made, whether it be animate or inanimate, is subject to failure. This applies to human organizations as well as to any other artifices. The CX depends upon its operators for its care and feeding, and, if it is neglected, not even its excellent bloodlines will exempt it from the laws of entropy.

Toner cartridge reloading

Toner cartridges as they were handed down from their maker were self-contained and self-sufficient, and said to be thoroughly disposable. When the toner supply was spent, the old cartridge was to be replaced by a factory-fresh recruit and then the retiree was to be quietly disposed of in a discreet manner. It was a ruthlessly neat and ultimately expensive plan that Canon had devised for the perpetual replenishment of "expendables." Of course, at least two things were wrong with that proposition, namely, that the cartridges were not entirely useless when the toner was gone, and that the people at Canon were notably more free with the customers' money than were the customers themselves. After all, does everybody buy a new automobile each time the gas tank runs dry? The toner cartridge was simply made too well to be thrown away after one use. The drum did not wear out as soon as Canon had hoped, and a scratched drum is the only valid excuse for wasting a cartridge. And you can always salvage something from such a used cartridge.

It is common nowadays to pick up a computer magazine and find advertisements for cartridge recharging services. Prices range from $35 to $50, depending upon the area of the country: The more competition, the lower the price. This is less than half of the cost of a new cartridge, while the blacks are almost always darker and the number of pages delivered higher from the refilled units. This is a very good deal, at least, for the reloader it is. Considering that the total amount of new material supplied can be purchased for less than $10 dollars, and that the total investment of time is less than 30 minutes, however, this is not such a good deal for the consumer. You can pay full price, half price, or a tenth of the price. You can also use dollar bills to line the bottom of the budgie's cage instead of yesterday's newspaper. Anyone can reload a toner cartridge.

First, some tools are needed. As usual, they can be as easy to find and as inexpensive as you care to make them, or they can be quite hard to get and rather more costly as a result. A Phillips screwdriver, a #10 Torx screwdriver, and a pair of flush snipping pliers are all that one actually needs for the task. The screwdrivers can be found in any hardware store. The pliers can be purchased at Sears Roebuck or Radio Shack. For the tool enthusiast, a pair of pin-pulling pliers has been manufactured especially. These have particularly thin pincers with which to loosen and pry out the plastic pins that fasten the cartridge together. They are a nice overrefinement since the ordinary ones serve as well.

The two methods to refill the CX toner cartridge are the "tear down," which is a complete disassembly, cleaning, and reload, and the "bore and burn," which involves either the drilling or burning of holes in the two toner reservoirs and omits the full cleaning. The tear down method is the one most likely to result in scratching of the photosensitive coating of the image drum, while the bore and burn method neglects the wear of certain elements of the cartridge that can cause premature failure. If you know how to tear down the cartridge, then that is the more satisfactory way to reload, for drum scratches can be avoided with a little caution in the removal of the toner tanks. The bore and burn method is quicker, and provides for easy reloading in subsequent operations, but it can result in leaky cartridges, residual scratching of the drum, and poor print quality if extreme care is not used in the first reload. Both methods are described and you can chose between them.

Bore and burn

The CX cartridge (Fig. C-1) has a cardboard label on the top, opposite the carrying handle, that bears instructions for preparing the cartridge for use and warnings against exposing it to extreme conditions of light, temperature, and humidity. The fresh toner tank reposes under this label and within the plastic shell of the cartridge itself. It is necessary, therefore, to remove the label before you can commence with the actual piercing of the tank. Do not expect to be able to reuse the label; it is glued securely in place and cannot be peeled off in one piece. A section of common cardboard of the same thickness can be substituted after the refilling has been completed.

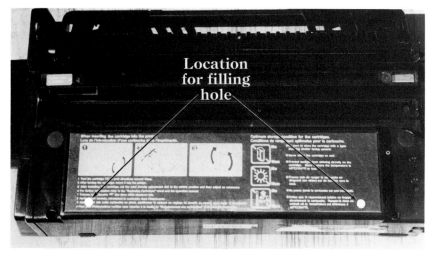

C-1   CX engine toner cartridge, top view.

Once the cardboard has been stripped away, the surface of the cartridge shell above the toner tank is exposed. Spread out a layer of newspaper on a table or workbench and lay the cartridge down in the middle. Choose a reasonably clean spot in the area from which the label was removed, preferably in a rear corner (Fig. C-1). This spot is where you will make the opening through which you will refill the tank. As always, you can choose your form of attack.

You can choose to burn the hole into the tank. This is probably the easiest way to go, because it requires only a hot soldering iron to accomplish. The soldering iron should have a conical tip and be of sufficient wattage to remain hot long enough to penetrate both the cartridge and tank in one attempt. The hole made should be about one quarter of an inch in diameter, or slightly larger than the diameter of the tip itself. It should be perfectly round, with no rough edges or filaments of plastic obstructing the hole. Be careful that no drops of molten plastic fall into the tank or onto your skin or clothing. Also, burning plastic produces fumes that can be toxic in large amounts, so be swift and sure in the melting of the hole.

If the soldering iron is not used, you must cut into the toner tank mechanically, either with a drill bit or a some other sharp instrument. A quarter inch speed bit will work, if you are prepared to drill upward. That is, the cartridge must be inverted, label side down, and the drill must approach from the underside, which means that the cartridge must be held or clamped above the drill. This is to ensure that no plastic chips or shavings fall into the tank, lest they later become mixed with the toner, causing scratching of the drum. An alternative is to find a Unibit™, which will drill a circular hole in the manner of a hole saw, taking out a plug of plastic rather than excavating the hole. This is a cleaner bit, creating fewer worrisome shavings, but it is wise to drill upward nonetheless. Do not sand or scrape the edges of the hole, but clean away all stray bits of plastic and abrasive plastic dust before proceeding.

Having made the hole, the fresh toner can then be poured into the tank. This can be done with a small funnel or by first putting the toner into a plastic squeeze bottle, such as a condiment dispenser with a pointed tip, and then emptying the squeeze bottle into the hole. Use the contents of one bottle of toner, about 250-300 grams.

Having filled the tank with new toner, the hole must be closed. If you have been an exacting worker, then you should be able to use a small metal cap plug which can be found in the hardware stores in an assortment of sizes (Fig. C-2). This snaps into the hole and seals it nicely. A rubber O-ring would make a good addition, however, to prevent leakage of toner into the printer, and it is a necessity if you have not made a perfectly round, smooth hole. If you prefer, the hole can also be sealed with tape, preferably a metallized tape with a strong adhesive. Some people find that the write-protect tabs supplied with 5 1/4 inch floppy disks make excellent seals.

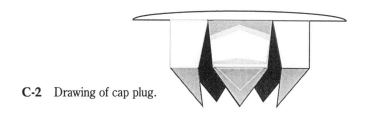

C-2 Drawing of cap plug.

With the toner refreshed, it remains to empty the spent toner from the tank located in the bottom front of the cartridge, just behind the handle and before the drum (Figs. C-3 and C-4). Here, drilling is the best way to breach the tank, because you must also pierce through a metal plate. You can enter at just about any point, but more forward from the drum rather than nearer is better, and on a smooth surface, not the ribbed area. This time the drilling can be done in a normal downward fashion, because the stray plastic and metal chips that might fall into the tank cannot later come into contact with drum. Therefore, drill a good size hole and then take the cartridge outside to empty the spent toner. This should be dumped into a plastic bag. It is best to draw the bag partially over the cartridge, covering the vent from which the toner is exiting while shaking the cartridge, so that neither you nor your surroundings are covered with escaping toner. It also helps if one or both of the Phillips screws is removed before the emptying is begun, giving air a place to enter the tank and thereby aiding in the smooth flow of the toner.

C-3 The spent toner tank.

With the spent toner removed, the hole can be sealed with a cap plug or tape, as you elect. As this hole is normally on the bottom of the cartridge when it is in place in the printer, this hole must be properly and securely sealed.

Next, it is a good idea to dust the drum with some drum conditioner, a powder that acts as a lubricant. Carefully draw back the shutter on the bottom of the cartridge to expose the drum. Remember that the drum should not receive strong illumination, nor should it be touched with the fingers or any hard object. A small bag or sack formed from a soft piece of cloth into which some conditioner has been tied can be the duster. Simply tamp the bag on the drum's surface. The drum can be rotated

C-4 Spent toner tank, in an exploded view.

by thumb pressure on the gears at the end of the drum. With the drum lightly dusted, the filling is complete. If you think it useful, the gauge on the end of the cartridge can be reset to the green to indicate a full cartridge.

The tear down

The tear down method of refilling is the one adopted by most commercial reloaders, because it is easier to spot defects and to detect wear of interior parts that can indicate that the cartridge has outlived its usefulness. If properly done, it runs no risk and entails no complications as does the drilling of the tanks.

There are two Torx head screws in the end of the cartridge's case where the use gauge is located (Fig. C-5). Remove these with the #15 (T-10) Torx screwdriver. (This same screwdriver can be used to open Macintoshes if one inch of the handle, as measured from where the shaft emerges, is ground down to allow clearance of the case.) The end of the cartridge should next be pried off by simultaneously depressing the locking tab and pulling on the end piece. A flatbladed screwdriver will do the job.

Under the cover as shown in Fig. C-6 is the red, yellow, and green dial of the cartridge use gauge (center), a large spring to the right (rear), a smaller spring left and above (forward), and a plastic lever that engages the drum shutter mechanism (center forward). Remove the two springs and the lever by slipping them off their plastic or metal shafts, and lay them aside. On this end of the cartridge housing are

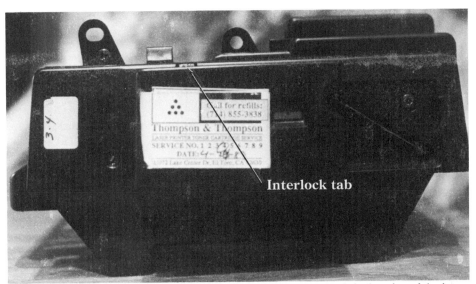

C-5 End of the cartridge case showing the rotating use gauge and the location of the inter-
lock tab.

three plastic pins or pegs (Fig. C-6), one directly in front of the metal plate on which
the use gauge is mounted, the second diagonally above to the front just beneath the
metal bracket at the top of the cartridge, and the third above the gauge itself. If the
cartridge has not been refilled before, these pins will have been lightly glued in place.
If so, loosen them with a thin, sharp knife blade, and then pull them with the pliers.
Be careful not to apply too much pressure with the pliers, else you will cut off the
heads of the pins. Lay the pins aside, and turn the cartridge end for end.

The other end of the cartridge (Fig. C-7) has two Phillips head screws and two
plastic pegs: Remove all. Next, lay the cartridge upside down and locate the two
Phillips head screws in the bottom of the spent toner tank (towards the handle).
Remove these screws.

On the gauge end of the cartridge, mounted on the drum shaft (Fig. C-6) is a
pinch spring that holds closed the drum shutter until the printer motor opens the
shutter to admit the paper. Disengage the end of the spring from the shutter by
pushing the spring forward and lifting until it clears the plastic tab against which it
normally rests. Relax the spring and allow it to open against the metal flange to the
rear.

At this point, you can remove the spent toner drum from the cartridge. Grasp it
at both ends and slide it forward and out (up), rotating it slightly as you lift so that it
follows the contour of the drum as it is removed. Lay the tank aside. Rotate the cartridge 180° and push open the shutter. (Remember the caution against bright light
on the drum.) Very carefully, insert a flat blade screwdriver into the gap between the
cartridge case and the white nylon gear on the end of the drum (Fig. C-4, center),

and apply sufficient pressure outwards to permit the raising of the end of the drum out of the case. Move the end of the drum forward and let it rest diagonally across the cartridge; the other end should remain in place. With extreme care, you can now slide out the fresh toner tank. Begin by lifting the left-hand end, and then slip the tank along the length of the drum until the gears on the right-hand end of the tank are clear of the drum, at which time the tank can be safely lifted out of the case. Be very careful that the gears do not touch and scratch the drum.

C-6 Location of plastic fastening pegs.

C-7 The other end of the cartridge.

The fresh toner tank, defying all logic for a supposedly disposable item, is built with a port through which it can be refilled (Fig. C-8). This is closed by a plastic stopper located on one end of the tank. However, the tank should be cleaned before refilling. Toner usually builds up along the edge where the metal roller within the drum dispenses the film of toner to the photosensitive drum. This residue should be wiped away with either a soft tissue or a soft bristled brush. The toner, as you might have noted, is strongly attracted to the metal roller. Do not tear the thin plastic film on the edge of the tank. The tank is then ready to be filled. The spent toner tank can be emptied simply by dumping its contents into a plastic bag.

C-8 With the cover removed, you can see the plastic stopper on the end of the "disposable" cartridge can be removed for refilling.

Reassembly of the cartridge proceeds in the reverse of the disassembly. Replace the fresh toner tank with as much caution as it was removed, sliding it into place. Return the drum to its normal position. Insert the spent toner tank with a rolling motion, and then close the drum shutter. The pegs and screws should be restored to their proper places, and the use gauge set to the green. The springs and the shutter lever are the last to be replaced before snapping on the end cover and putting in the two Torx screws. Apply the drum lubricant and the toner cartridge is ready to be put back into service. It can be expected to last about 20% longer, on average, than a new cartridge, and the print quality should be better.

The last thing to do before starting the printer is to install a new lubricated felt into the fusion roller cleaning wand. Usually the rechargers supply a replacement wand, which is exchanged for the old wand. The end user, however, can simply scrape out the old felt and introduce a new one. The felts come with the silicone oil already applied, and there is generally a self-sticking adhesive on the back that is covered with a paper protector, after the manner of two-sided tape or two- sided sticky paper.

It is almost an afterthought, but the small corona cleaning tool that comes with the printer (Fig. C-9) should be used on the cartridge corona. It fits into the slot on the top of the cartridge (Fig. C-10) and ought to be lightly rubbed back and forth over the corona to keep it clean. With that, the reload is complete.

Toner types

Toner is sold for the CX engine in massive lots, which distributors divide into discrete loads of approximately 225 – 250 grams. They can be purchased in two grades, normal toner and graphic's toner. Normal toner is used for general purpose printing that is text intensive, and graphic's toner is formulated to produce richer, more even blacks for graphic intensive usages. The normal reloads are frequently rated for more pages than the graphic's toner reloads. Of course, you can increase the density of the print of the normal toner, while reducing the page count, merely by setting the print density dial to a lower number. It is noteworthy that toner can be obtained in three colors, black, blue, and brown, and cartridges can be reloaded with any color if first they are thoroughly cleaned.

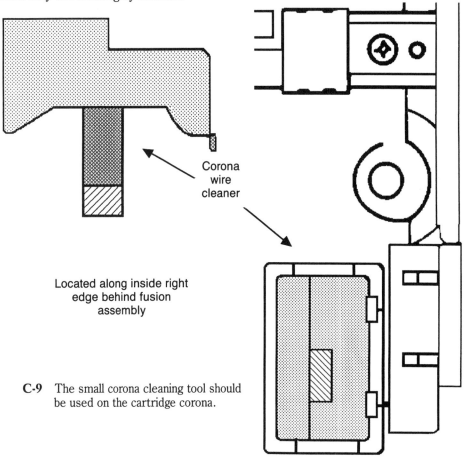

Corona
wire
cleaner

Located along inside right
edge behind fusion
assembly

C-9   The small corona cleaning tool should
be used on the cartridge corona.

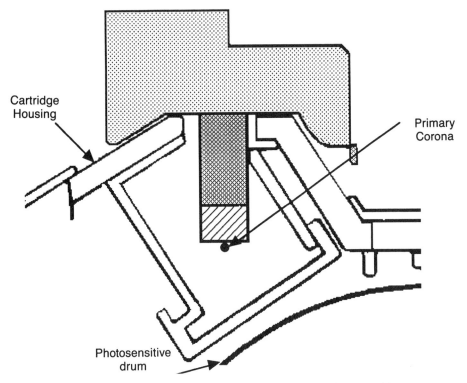

Cartridge
Housing

Primary
Corona

Photosensitive
drum

C-10   The corona wire cleaner fits in the top slot of the cartridge.

Lastly, make certain that the toner purchased is for the CX laser engine, not for the SX or the Canon line of copiers. The toners are all different and incompatible.

Cleaning

You can begin housekeeping with that inconspicuous but ubiquitous paper dust that collects in the bed of the printer. It should be periodically blown or otherwise harried out of the crevices and corners of the lower half of the printer. It can, in quantity, cause smudging and skipping of the printed page as it accumulates and adheres to the paper, interfering with the fusion process. It can also be conductive and cause mischief around the high voltage discharges within the printer.

Occasionally, it is a good idea to gently wipe the fusion rollers with a moist cloth (Fig. 1-6) to remove any paper dust or toner that might have been deposited. Do not clean when hot, and make certain that all moisture has evaporated before closing the printer.

The corona wire in the bed of the printer needs to be wiped with a cotton swab every 3000 pages or so (Fig. C-11). The swab should be dampened with a little isopropyl alcohol and lightly run along the nearly invisible wire. This prevents the accumulation of oxides that could degrade the corona effect.

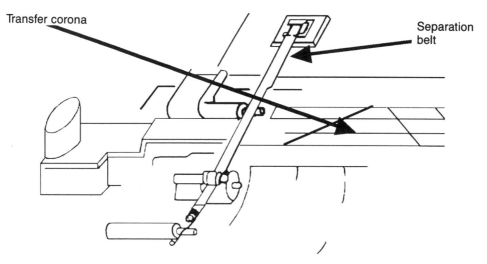

C-11 Location of transfer corona and separation belt.

Incidentally, a side effect of the corona effect is the production of ozone, which, while it does nothing to close the holes in the upper polar atmosphere, is concentrated enough that the printer incorporates an activated charcoal filter to absorb the gas. This should last the life of the printer without being changed, although, if you were to smell what seemed like excessive amounts of the pungent gas, it might be wise to check the filter. It is located in the upper portion of the printer, and can be reached by removing the toner cartridge and looking up into the underside or roof of the cartridge cavity (Fig. C-12).

On the left-hand end of the transfer corona assembly is a small strip of transparent plastic stretched from a spring (running in the front to back direction). This is the separation belt that peels the charged, toner covered paper from the drum. This belt can be cleaned with a moist cloth from time to time, or if stains appear on the paper edge. (See the section on troubleshooting.) This belt is the reason that you cannot print to the edge of the page, because the belt would smear any toner image that extended into that area. The life of the belt is rated at 50,000 pages and breakage can be expected during the life of the printer. A replacement is supplied (Fig. C-20) with a new printer or can be purchased from Hewlett-Packard in a service kit, part number 92285T. The kit also includes fusion wiper pads.

Troubleshooting

Most of the problems that will arise during the normal operation of the printer will be manifested as print defects (Fig. C-13), and many of these can be corrected by the user. However, if the corrective procedures do not remedy the defects, a service technician might be required. The following are the most frequently encountered page defects as listed by Hewlett-Packard in their service manuals (HP 2686A/D

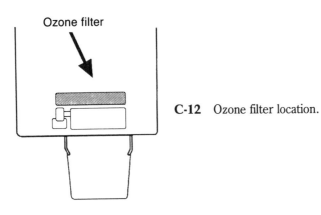

Ozone filter

C-12 Ozone filter location.

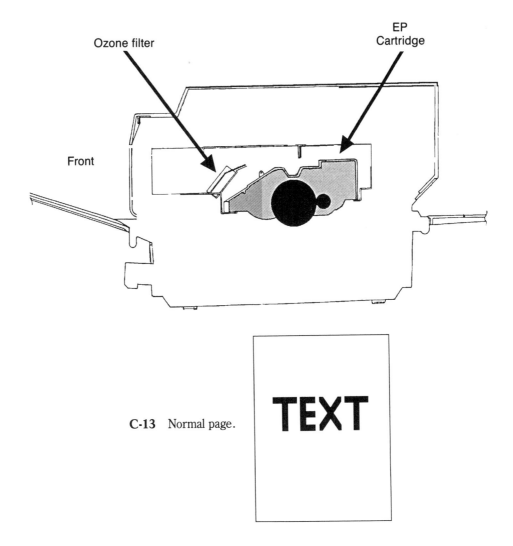

Ozone filter

EP
Cartridge

Front

C-13 Normal page.

TEXT

LaserJet Printer Service Manual, revised edition, part number 02686-90920, available from HP's Direct Marketing Division for $29).

Print skewing

Print skewing (Figs. C-14 and C-16) is defined by misalignment of the printed text on the page relative to the paper edges. An unevenness of the print borders from top to bottom or from side to side on either the horizontal or vertical text boundaries, as displayed in the difference shown between border a and border b in Fig. C-14, with the lines of text parallel to the edges of the paper but with the margins unequal, can be corrected by refitting the paper fence in the paper cassette (Fig. C-15). Two screws hold the fence on the bottom of the cassette. Loosen, but do not remove, these screws. Place a stack of paper in the cassette and make it flush against the side of the cassette. Move the paper fence until the Velcro pad is touching the paper stack and is evenly aligned. Tighten the screws.

The second type of misalignment, as shown in Fig. C-16, with the lines of text parallel to one another and to the top and bottom margins but not to the paper's edges, is caused by the laser scanning unit. Adjustment of the laser scanning mechanism is possible, but it involves working on the printer while it is operating. Therefore, you are advised to consult either a technician or to familiarize yourself with the HP service manual (section 5-4) before making the adjustment. Operating the printer while the laser unit is being worked on can be hazardous.

Light printing

A faint or low contrast image on a white background (Fig. C-17) can be caused by several faults, the most common being the lack of toner in the cartridge and the setting of the print density dial to a too high number. If the use gauge of the toner cartridge is in the red, then rocking of the cartridge from side to side to redistribute the remaining toner can often extend the page count. Otherwise, replace or refill the cartridge. The print density dial is inversely numbered with regard to darkness of the image, a higher number representing a lower primary corona voltage and consequently fainter image. Adjust the dial to a lower setting.

Another cause of a light image can be the type of paper used. Paper with high moisture absorbency can become damp and therefore not bind the image properly. Use high quality laser or copier grade paper.

If none of the above mentioned potential sources of trouble seems to be the cause of the light image, then it is possible that the laser power is insufficient, the high voltage power supply is weak, or grid bias is not at optimum (about $-690V$). These faults must be checked for and repaired by a qualified technician.

C-14 Paper skewing due to cassette misalignment.

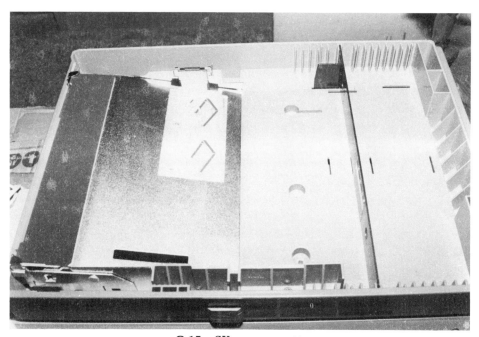

C-15 CX paper cassette.

Dark printing

Dark printing (Fig. C-18), wherein areas that should be white are gray and text appears blocked, can be corrected in most cases by adjusting the print density to a higher setting. If, however, the maximum setting is required to eliminate the background graying, then the high voltage printed circuit assembly might be defective. Diagnosis and replacement should be done by a qualified technician.

C-16 Paper skewing due to laser scanning misalignment.

C-17 A light page.

C-18 A dark page.

Right edge staining

A vertical staining or striping along the length of the right edge of the page can be caused by a dirty separation belt (Fig. C-19). The separation belt (Fig. C-20), separation roller, and pinch roller should all be examined and cleaned.

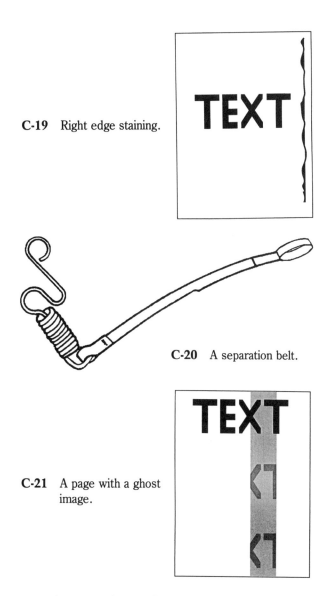

C-19   Right edge staining.

C-20   A separation belt.

C-21   A page with a ghost
image.

Ghost images and vertical streaks in print area

The appearance of ghost images (Fig. C-21) in a gray, vertical stripe within the printing area of the page is usually caused by wearing of the cleaner blade in the EP cartridge. When this occurs, replace the cartridge.

Horizontal lines

Horizontal lines (Fig. C-22) that appear at regular intervals (approximately 188 mm or 66 mm) down the length of the page are the result of defects in the photosensitive drum. Replacing the cartridge or resurfacing of the drum are the only solutions.

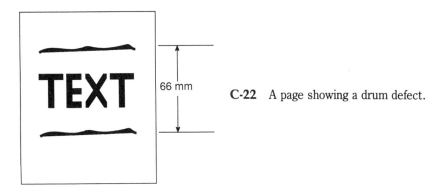

C-22 A page showing a drum defect.

Tinkering tips

This is an agglomeration of heterogeneous bits of knowledge that you might or might not find useful, but that I find interesting. If you purchase the Hewlett-Packard Service and Repair Manuals for the LaserJets, you will find these small surprises hidden away in odd corners of the text, where they might be easily passed over without notice.

It is one of the annoying facts of CX laser ownership, that Canon designed the paper cassettes to hold any standard size of paper, but then "fixed" it so that each cassette was limited to one paper size and one alone. Even if the rear paper fence were to be moved back in a letter size cassette in order to accommodate legal size pages, the printer would still treat the paper inserted as letter size and would indicate a paper jam as the longer paper passed through the pick-up mechanism. This has forced many purchases of multiple paper cassettes by those who frequently use more than one size of paper and who do not wish to single feed reams through the manual feed paper path. Hewlett-Packard has been a beneficiary of this single-minded cassette sizing scheme, but HP also provides you with the information necessary to circumvent the purchase of extra cassettes.

On the side of the ordinary letter-size paper cassettes are three plastic ribs (Fig. C-23). These ribs are not ornamental, they are functional. They engage three micro-switches in the wall of the paper cassette bay, the states of which are coded to translate for the printer the type of paper being used in the installed cassette. Table C-1 shows the interpretation of the switch positions. Note that the switches are high when open and low when closed or active.

By manipulating the states of the switches, it is possible to fool or defeat the paper size sensors. There being but one switch condition separating the legal from the letter size cassette, you can remove the third (bottom) tab from the letter-size tray and move the rear paper fence into the legal size position. Converting in both directions between the two sizes requires taping or otherwise temporarily refitting the tab to the cassette and then removing the tab as necessary. Or you can purchase a second tray for $50.

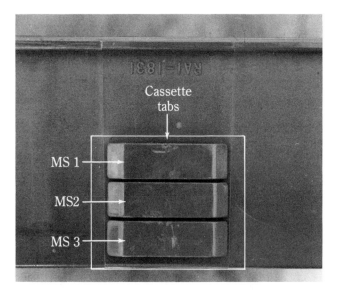

C-23 Paper cassette size tabs.

Table C-1. Interpretation of the switch positions.

Micro-Switch	Condition						
5	high	high	high	low	low	low	low
6	high	high	low	low	low	high	high
7	high	low	low	low	high	low	high
Paper size	No cassette	Not used	B5	Letter	Legal	A4	N

Similarly, the rear of the toner cartridge has sensitivity tabs that are set at the time of manufacture to denote the degree of photosensitivity of the drum coating, namely, whether it is high (highly conductive), medium (moderately or normally conductive), or low (less conductive than normal).

These tabs (Fig. C-24) are located on the left rear corner of the cartridge and are coded in a manner identical to that of the paper size switch tabs. Thus, an open switch generates a high state and a closed switch generates a low state. Table C-2 shows the relationship of the switch states to the drum sensitivity.

These settings are detected by the Machine Control System of the printer and are used inversely to select the proper high voltage charge for the primary corona. The lower the drum's sensitivity, the higher must be the charge imparted by the corona to achieve uniform results. Therefore, if you are unsatisfied with the print density that is being delivered by the cartridge in use, and a lower print density setting does not correct the lightness, you can induce an even higher corona voltage by removing both tabs from the cartridge. This is rarely, if ever, necessary, however, because darker toners and a denser setting of the print density dial almost always produce the desired blackness.

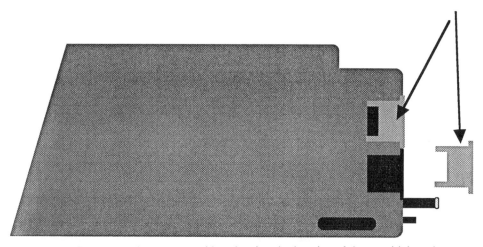

C-24 Rear view of a toner cartridge showing the location of the sensitivity tabs.

**Table C-2. The relationship of the
switch states to the drum sensitivity.**

Micro-switch	Condition		
3	open	closed	closed
4	open	open	closed
Sensitivity	Low	Moderate	High

A third tip that is useful primarily to the purchaser of used equipment, is that you can determine a rough page count for the machine by inspecting the page counter that is part of every CX engine. This is a small tube, resembling a common automotive or electronic fuse, demarcated into decades of pages (10,000 pages each), with a mercury indicator that migrates along the demarcations to show an approximate number of pages processed by the printer. The page counter is located inside the upper portion of the main body, above the ozone filter (Fig. C-12). After the filter has been removed, the erase lamps should be visible. The page counter is on the underside of the lamp assembly. You read the page count from left to right. This is useful to verify the seller's page count and to determine if the engine is in need of an overhaul. Unfortunately, this is not a foolproof counter: Like the odometer of an automobile, the counter can be reset to a lower number, this by simply reversing the counter in its holder if it is beyond the midpoint.

Finally, for those who are using computers that do not support PostScript directly from software, or who are using software that must print to a device other than a PostScript printer, there is hope. The Apple LaserWriter Manual contains PostScript programs that, when downloaded into the LaserWriter, allow the printer to emulate the Hewlett-Packard LaserJet, the Diablo 630 Daisy wheel printer, or the

Apple ImageWriter. This is certainly underutilization, but there do arise unusual circumstances in which such extreme measures are necessary. Also, for users of Apple II or compatible computers, Apple supplies a ready-to-use ImageWriter emulator on disk as part of the Apple IIGS system software. This text file can be modified to provide practically any type of printer emulation if you have the PostScript programming knowledge and the needed printer codes for the type of printer to be emulated.

Bibliography

LaBadie, Horace W., Jr. "Boys! Grow Giant LaserWriters in Your Basements!," *Computer Shopper*, January 1990, pp. 378-379, 680.

Lancaster, Don. "Ask the Guru" and "LaserWriter Corner," *Computer Shopper*.

   August 1986 (Toner cartridge reloading)
   November 1986 (LaserWriter password problems)
   February 1987 (Toner cartridge reloading)
   March 1987 (LaserWriter/PostScript grays)
   December 1987 (AppleTalk, LaserWriter halftone gray map)
   January 1988 (AppleTalk substitute connectors)
   November 1988 (LaserWriter cables)
   February 1989 (SX toner cartridge reloading)
   April 1989 (High speed, 57,600 baud, LaserWriter communications)

Reprints of "Ask the Guru" columns are available in bound volumes directly from Don Lancaster by writing to Synergetics, Box 809, Thatcher, AZ 85552, or calling (602)-428-4073.

Saulsbury, Greg. "Building A Low-Cost PostScript Laser Printer," *Computer Shopper*, June 1989, pp. 241 – 245, 407, 410. Contact Greg Saulsbury for documentation on LaserJet conversion at Custom Technology, 192 Lakeshore Drive, Texarkana, TX 75501.

Index

V

video cable
  IDC pin placement, 32
  replacing, 31
video interface cables, 35

W

Warnock, John, xvii
wiper pad, 4
wiring, 118
  interface, 26-37

Other Bestsellers of Related Interest

BUILD YOUR OWN 80486 PC AND SAVE A BUNDLE—Aubrey Pilgrim

With inexpensive third-party components and clear, step-by-step photos and assembly instructions—and without any soldering, wiring, or electronic test instruments—you can assemble a 486. This book discusses boards, monitors, hard drives, cables, printers, modems, faxes, UPSs, memory, floppy disks, and more. It includes parts lists, mail order addresses, safety precautions, troubleshooting tips, and a glossary of terms. 240 pages, 62 illustrations. **Book No. 3628, $26.95 hardcover only**

ROGER HAINES ON HVAC CONTROLS —Roger W. Haines

Instantly put your finger on any piece of advice from Haines' popular monthly column in *Heating/Piping/Air Conditioning Magazine*. Permanent, accessible, and fully indexed, this reference compiles nearly 50 articles. You can access Haines' most popular articles on philosophy, theory, systems and subsystems, control devices, and computer-based control systems. He gives you easy-to-understand, practical advice on a wide range of topics. 240 pages, 158 illustrations. **Book No. 3625, $36.95 hardcover only**

WORDPERFECT® 5.1 MACROS —Donna M. Mosich, Robert Bixby, and Pamela Adams-Regan

Get everything you need to know about macros in any version of WordPerfect through 5.1. Create and use macros to generate form letters, automate mailing list production, index manuscripts, and more! There are more than 300 usable macros covered in this guide (and available on disk), with explanations and illustrations on how the macro command language is used. 480 pages, 162 illustrations. **Book No. 3617, $26.95 paperback, $34.95 hardcover**

STRATEGY, SYSTEMS, AND INTEGRATION: A Handbook for Information Managers —George M. Hall

Now you can successfully plan new data processing systems and integrate existing systems. Hall shows you how you can get beyond basic strategic problems and concentrate on mastering the techniques that will meet the increasing demands of your system. From an in-depth analysis of database requirements to key management issues, you'll follow the logical order in which systems should be designed and developed. 384 pages, 118 illustrations. **Book No. 3614, $39.95 hardcover only**

THE DOS CONSTRUCTION KIT
—James S. Forney

Discover the professional tricks and secrets that make DOS less intimidating. And set up and manage a customized operating system following the techniques outlined in this easy-to-use guidebook. Find out how to weigh your utility options, avoid compatibility traps, optimize DOS shells, enhance applications performance, work beyond the 640K barrier, and more, with the help of DOS expert Forney. 384 pages, Illustrated. **Book No. 3563, $22.95 paperback only**

AUTOCAD™ Methods and Macros
2nd Edition—Jeff Guenther and Ed Ocoboc

With 275 illustrations, this completely revised and updated guide takes you step by step through dozens of useful techniques for working through Release 11 of AutoCAD. Twenty new chapters outline object selection, lines, editing, and viewing documents, inserting drawings into documents, working with text, sketching, printer plots, dialogue boxes, the new multi-purpose menu, and much more. 464 pages, 275 illustrations. **Book No. 3544, $34.95 hardcover only**

MS-DOS® BATCH FILE PROGRAMMING
2nd Edition—Ronny Richardson

Reviewer's praise of the first edition:
"By the end of this book, readers will be able to implement even the most difficult batch files, and will thoroughly understand the whole process.

—Computer Shopper

Now, even the novice can take advantage of batch files—simple step-saving programs that can replace complicated DOS procedures. Includes DOS 4 and the latest in batch utilities. Comes with a disk containing all the batch files. 448 pages, 339 illustrations. **Book No. 3537, $36.95 hardcover only**

XYWRITE™ REVEALED
—Herbert L. Tyson

This book clearly explains one of the fastest and most powerful word processing programs ever. It helps you customize the program, and spells out XyWrite's powerful but undocumented features. Learn never-before-published techniques for keyboard and printer files, editing functions, the help system, advanced save/gets, debugging tools, search and replace, default settings, file sort, formatting, file storage, tables, and column display. 456 pages 76 illustrations. **Book No. 3459, $34.95 hardcover only**

MICROCOMPUTER LANs—2nd Edition
—Michael Hordeski

Pull together a multi-user system from your stand-alone micros. With this book, you gain an understanding of how networking actually happens. This comprehensive source helps you make the right decisions and cut through the confusion surrounding LAN technology and performance. You'll evaluate your alternatives intelligently, set up networks that allow for growth, restructure or upgrade LAN configurations, and effectively manage network systems. 384 pages, 135 illustrations. **Book No. 3424, $39.95 hardcover only**

BUILDING C LIBRARIES—Len Dorfman

Improve the quality of your programs while drastically reducing development time with this new guide from expert Len Dorfman. He shows you how to use the library manager to create your own professional window, screen, and keyboard handling libraries. *Building C Libraries* emphasizes interfaces and library development. You get line after line of well-documented source code for menus, pop-up windows, Macintosh-style pull-downs, bounce bars, and more. 432 pages, 198 illustrations. **Book No. 3418, $26.95 paperback, $34.95 hardcover**

EXPLORING PARALLEL PROCESSING
—Edward Rietman

Overcome the barriers that hold down your computing speed and start on the processing of the future. Complete with practical examples you can use right away, Rietman's book is a look at all the strategies currently under study for parallel processing. It is liberally illustrated with programs and models in BASIC and C. This book also explains how to use three powerful add-in boards. 288 pages, 190 illustrations. **Book No. 3367, $18.95 paperback only**

COMPUTER TECHNICIAN'S HANDBOOK
3rd Edition—Art Margolis

This is a clear book, with concise and sensible language and lots of large diagrams . . . use [it] to cure or prevent problems in [your] own system . . . the [section on troubleshooting and repair] is worth the price of the book."

—Science Software Quarterly

More than just a how-to-manual of do-it yourself fix-it techniques, this book offers complete instructions on interfacing and modification that will help you get the most out of your PC. 579 pages, 97 illustrations. **Book No. 3279, $36.95 hardcover only**

80386 MACRO ASSEMBLER AND TOOLKIT
—Penn Brumm and Don Brumm

Expand your programming horizons with this guide to writing and using assembly language on 80386-based computers with Microsoft Macro Assembler (MASM), 5.1. This collection of useful macros illustrates the concepts presented. There is also a detailed discussion of MASM syntax and grammer, plus coverage of the options and their usage. 608 pages, 284 illustrations. **Book No. 3247, $35.95 hardcover only**

NETWORKING WITH BANYAN® VINES®
—Edwin G. Laubach

Master the sophisticated Banyan VINES software with this practical approach to networking. Laubach offers essential guidelines for setting up and using an effective VINES operation. Anyone from the first-time network builder to the experienced VINES user will find tips and practical examples throughout the text, including: network topologies, Street-Talk protocols, creating groups and services, wiring centers, maintenance and disaster recovery, and more. 336 pages, 88 illustrations. **Book No. 3405, $21.95 paperback only**

COMPUTER VIRUSES: What They Are, How They Work, and How to Avoid Them—Jonathan L. Mayo

The Trojan horse, the worm, and the logic bomb—all these are programs that move silently from computer to computer, destroying and changing files. Now you can protect your computer from these and other ailments. Mayo explains how viruses get into your computer and examines the parts of DOS that are most susceptible to infection. With this book you'll receive a disk containing some of the best shareware and public domain anti-viral programs available, including top-rated Flu_Shot +! 176 pages, 40 illustrations, Book/Disk Combo. **Book No. 3382, $29.95 paperback only**

**FIBER OPTIC COMMUNICATIONS
HANDBOOK
2nd Edition—Technical Staff of CSELT,
Edited by Federico Tosco**
Find the detailed theory, practical data,
and in-depth references you need to design,
produce, install, and operate a cost-effective,
dynamic fiber optics communications system.
With over 800 illustrations, you'll discover
state-of-the-art information on transmission
media and systems, optical cables and passive
devices, systems, integrated optics, non-linear
fiber optics, and phototonic communications.
1,200 pages, 820 illustrations. **Book No. 3201,
$89.50 hardcover only**

Quick troubleshooting check

Symptom	Check point
Nothing happens. Printer engine motor does not start.	Check main power cord connections at wall and printer. Check auxiliary power supply connections at board and AC taps.
Engine motor starts, but no test page is ejected. Interface Green LED on mode switch remains on or does not illuminate.	Check power supply voltage. Adjust to +5 volts, 3 amps. No light indicates logic board fault. Check interface cable orientation. Flip cable end connector if necessary.
Interface LED shows normal, but no test page. Status LEDs appear normal.	Check video interface cable connections for continuity from J-202 on DC controller to logic board.
Yellow busy LED does not flash.	Disconnect logic board from DC controller. Power up printer. When Green warm-up status LED has ceased flashing, press Test button to print test pattern. If page prints, probable logic board fault is indicated. No test pattern indicates DC controller fault.
Normal startup but no response from printer to computer.	Check cabling between printer and computer. Turn off printer and disconnect cable to computer. Turn printer on and wait until startup page has been printed, then reconnect cabling. Check communications protocol in software (serial). Check AppleTalk connections and Chooser settings (AppleTalk/LocalTalk). Continued failure indicates probable serial interface fault in printer logic board.
Print skewing.	Check cassette and cassette fence alignment.
Dark/Light printing	Set Print density dial to higher/lower number.
Repeat stray marks.	Check EP cartridge for scratches.